The Venison Kitchen
by Anona Gow

Damsah /
Spiced
Ginger Venison
- orange peppes
- red onion
- ginger
- garam
  masala
- cinnamon

Copyright

This book is published by Grosvenor House Publishing Ltd Link House, 140 The Broadway, Tolworth, Surrey, KT6 7HT. www.grosvenorhousepublishing.co.uk

A CIP record for this book is available from the British Library.

ISBN 978-1-80381-944-0

To all the wonderful farmers, estate owners, gamekeepers and stalkers who dedicate their lives to looking after our spectacular countryside and our tremendous array of animals – you are inspirational to us all.

Introduction

I am a busy working Mum so quick, simple recipes that make a scrumptious meal are essential and this book is full of mealtime winners from cosy suppers to dinner party showstoppers!

Venison is a sustainable, healthy red meat and the good news is you don't have to be a fancy cordon bleu chef to cook it. I am a self-taught, farmhouse cook so can relate to everyone at home who is keen to create dishes which are exciting and different but not too tricky.

Historically, Venison was seen as an expensive, luxury meat but happily, it is now accessible to all and readily available from both supermarkets and farmers markets alike – although I would always recommend buying from your local producer.

A naturally lean meat, Venison provides a fantastic alternative to other red meats as it is low in fat, low in calories and helpful for those on low cholesterol diets as it is lower in fat and cholesterol than skinless chicken. Venison has higher iron levels than other red meats and is a valuable source of essential Omega 3 fatty acids.

Offering so many different cuts, Venison is incredibly versatile and is happily married to traditional flavours as it is with more modern, dynamic flavours and ingredients. It is no longer the old-fashioned meat of game hunters and I am passionate about encouraging people to use it whether it is in simple recipes like Lasagne or experimenting with spices from the Orient or the Middle East.

I promise, if I can do these recipes, then you can too, so pour yourself a glass of something delicious and have a go!

Butchery Cuts

NECK

SHOULDER

FILLET / LOIN

FILET MIGNON

FLANK

HAUNCH

SHANK

SHANK

My Golden Rules for Cooking Venison

The most important aspect to remember when cooking Venison is to cook it according to the cut.

For lean cuts like fillet and steaks always think: **Less is More**

For cuts like casserole and shanks, always think: **Long and Low**

FILLETS: a fillet should be seared in a hot pan for around three to four minutes on each side depending on how thick it is and left for eight to ten minutes to rest. It will be rare and scrumptious – if however you like it a little less pink you will have to leave it another minute or two.

HAUNCH STEAKS: these need to be seared in a hot pan for one and a half minutes each side, then leave to rest for five minutes and they will be lovely and pink in the middle.

FILLET MIGNON: this is the finest cut from the beastie and just requires a maximum of two minutes on each side, then leave it to rest for five minutes or so, delicious!

MINUTE STEAKS: these really just need to be shown the pan – by the time you have put four in the pan you need to turn the first one. Twenty to thirty seconds a side will do it!

MINCE: Venison mince browns like all minces but again, as there is less fat, it browns quicker so watch out for it sticking and over cooking.

ROAST HAUNCH: again, due to the low-fat content, be careful not to let the Venison dry out when roasting. Brown the joint first then cook for ten to twelve mins per 450g for rare/medium and twelve to fourteen mins per 450g for medium to well done. Do baste it if you wish.

ROAST SHOULDER: this cut needs to be cooked long and low with plenty of delicious juices so brown it first in a pan with olive oil then add the ingredients as per the recipe suggestion with all the juices, cover tightly and cook at a low temperature for as long as possible. This cut is perfect for slow cookers.

SHANKS: these need to be browned in a hot pan then cooked long and low with lots of delicious sauce. Again, slow cookers work well with this cut.

CASSEROLE: once bubbling, these chunks usually require around four to six hours in the simmering oven with lots of lovely sauce and juices. If you can pop it in your slow cooker, you will have a delicious meal waiting for you.

Deer Beasties

Venison is a sustainable red meat which is of course our national meat here in Scotland. There are six types of deer in the UK of which Red and Fallow are the only farmed deer beasties. Red, Roe, Sika, Fallow, Muntjac and Chinese Water Deer are found living wild across the UK.

Venison is widely available at affordable prices from deer farms, farm shops and increasingly supermarkets throughout the UK.

I am passionate about encouraging people to eat Venison, be it farmed or wild and it is important to understand the difference. Wild deer are just that, wild beasties roaming over land seeking food and shelter.

Farmed deer are generally culled when they are around 2 years old so their meat has a more gentle, consistent flavour and the animals have full traceability.

How an animal tastes is reflected in what it eats – there is a difference between those beasties eating plain hillside fodder and that of a deer with access to good grass and additional feed over the lean Winter months. On our farm we feed our deer potatoes and even our windfall apples and pears from the garden – those lucky beasties!

If you have ever heard someone say they don't like Venison, I suspect they have eaten an old wild beastie and would strongly encourage trying farmed Venison instead.

Animal husbandry, as with all farming, is key as it has a direct impact on the quality of the final product. Those beasties who have been well looked after and culled kindly and thoughtfully, will always taste better.

I would encourage you to eat as local as you can so try to purchase your Venison from a local farmers market or even better from your nearest Venison farm or estate.

Farmers all over the UK need our support now more than ever, particularly when we may soon be faced with a meat market, flooded with cheap foreign imports from countries which do not adhere to our rigorous standards, so please do buy British as much as you can afford.

Before we start

I am a self-taught cook and like so many, juggle work with looking after a family and doing chores so I am always keen to keep cooking simple but still scrumptious!

Whenever I can find a shortcut or easy way of doing something I will definitely take it and I hope you find some of my tips are useful.

Before starting your delicious Venison cooking journey, I just want to confirm the following bits of info:

1. Pans: lots of my recipes use a heavy bottomed pan with a tight-fitting lid – I use Le Creuset as they work perfectly every time but any similar pan will do. For searing meat I like to use a heavy bottomed griddle pan. Non stick deep pans with lids are also a vital piece of kitchen kit.

2. Measurements: I don't like weighing ingredients as I simply don't have the time so I tend to use spoons. In my recipes I have used the usual abbreviations: tbsp for tablespoon, tsp for teaspoon etc.

3. If you are a true domestic god or goddess, you will be keen to make your own Bechamel sauce or curry pastes. Sometimes, due to lack of time, I don't – please try not to judge me but do make your own if you wish.

4. Do bear in mind I cook on an Aga so make sure you read the temperature information overleaf.

5. Always make sure your Venison is at room temperature before you start cooking to ensure it remains succulent.

6. Keep your stopwatch handy as with the leaner cuts of Venison it is essential to time your cooking accurately so that it does not spoil and overcook.

7. Seasoning: I don't say "season to taste" in each recipe as I am assuming you will all do this as a matter of course. I always use freshly ground black pepper and pink Himalayan salt as we buy it in bulk and even give it to the deer as a lick due to its high mineral content – those lucky beasties!

8. Stock: of course it is always best to use homemade stock and if you do have the chance (and time) to make your own then fabulous, use that stock. However, if you don't have the time or inclination to do so then use the best stock you can buy as this will enhance the dish.

9. Portion size: what feeds the 4 of us may not feed your family, so please remember to amend the portion sizes accordingly.

Oven Temperatures

I feel incredibly lucky as I inherited an Aga in my kitchen so don't really think about actual temperatures and instead use a Roasting Oven, Baking Oven, Simmering Oven (which is like a slow cooker) and Warming Oven.

I appreciate that not everyone has this luxury so I have noted the rough oven equivalent temperatures opposite.

As those with Aga's know, every single one is slightly different and mine is a particularly old lady who is still going strong but her temperature does fluctuate a bit!

Roasting/Hot Oven:

240-260C	475-500F	Gas 8-9

Baking Oven:

180-200C	350-400F	Gas 4-6

Simmering Oven:

135-150C	260-300F	Gas 1

Warming Oven:

70-100C	150-200F	Gas ¼

When searing Venison fillets or steaks I tend to brown it on the Hot Plate (which boils a kettle) so it needs a hot hob.

For casseroles and shanks, I would brown the meat first then add the other ingredients and once bubbling, I would place in the simmering oven. The simmering oven can be used as a slow cooker and sometimes I even leave pans cooking in there overnight.

Recipes

Page 22

Page 25

Page 26

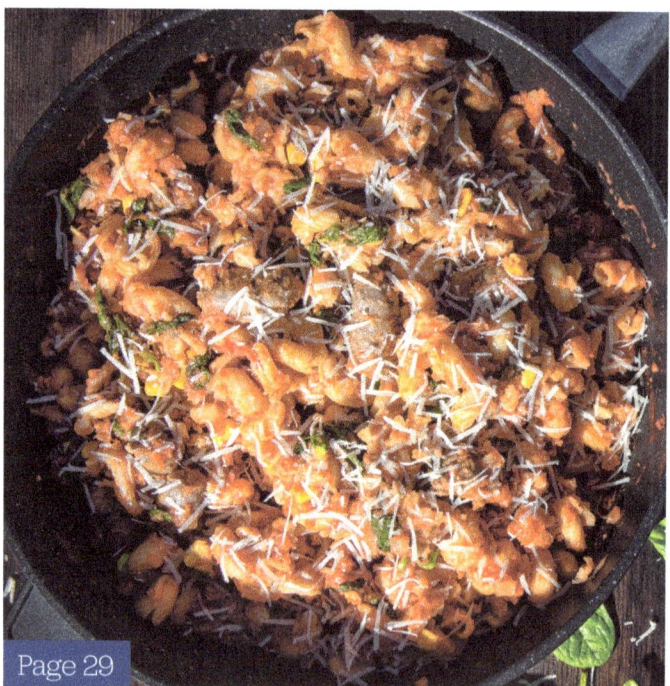

Page 29

Sausages

Venison sausages are simply scrumptious – our family adore them as they
are brilliant on the BBQ, roasted in the Aga or zhuzhed up for supper.
Your local butcher will no doubt have a lovely selection of
Venison sausages for you to choose from or, even better, go along to
your local farmers market and buy direct from your local producer.

Everyday Venison Sausages

Serves 4 to 6 people

- 12-16 Venison sausages (depending on who you are feeding!)
- 1 tablespoon of sunflower oil
- Seasoning

Method:

1. Take a roasting tray and pop in the sunflower oil, add the venison sausages and ensure you mix them well so they are evenly coated in oil.

2. Pop in the roasting oven of the Aga for 20 mins, turning them half way through.

3. For a quick, delicious lunch, serve them in a freshly buttered roll – scrumptious.

You may prefer to fry them – the method is the same, just ensure you fry them for 20 minutes turning them occasionally so they are a deep nutty brown on all sides.

Summer Sausage Casserole

This is a fantastic one pot recipe using delicious and healthy Venison sausages. As you will see, I use peppers and courgettes but really you can use whichever vegetables you prefer. This really is an easy recipe, so grab a glass of something yummy, (maybe just taste the cider to check it is OK) and get cracking.

Serves 4 - 6

- 12-16 Venison sausages, halved, widthways
- 1 tbsp olive oil
- 1 red onion halved and finely sliced
- 120g chorizo, diced
- 3 garlic cloves peeled and crushed
- 1 tbsp flour
- 4 tsp grainy French mustard
- $^1/_2$ a courgette cut into 1 inch chunks
- $^1/_2$ a red pepper cut into 1 inch chunks
- 12 small new potatoes cut in half
- 500ml apple cider
- 100ml double cream
- 1 tbsp fresh coriander, finely chopped to serve

Method:

1. Pop the olive oil, red onion, garlic and chorizo into a heavy based pan (which has a tight-fitting lid) on the simmering plate and gently sizzle, stirring occasionally.

2. When you see the lovely red juices coming out of the chorizo, add in the halved sausages and brown them all over.

3. When they are a lovely nutty brown, sprinkle over the plain flour and mix well.

4. Now add in the mustard and mix well.

5. Add the chopped vegetables and potatoes then cover with the cider and bring to the boil. Leave uncovered on the simmering plate for 10 minutes allowing it to bubble and reduce the sauce by about a third.

6. Pop the lid on the pan and transfer it to the baking oven for 40 minutes.

7. Bring the pan out and check the potatoes are cooked. If they are and you are ready to eat, add in the cream (add more if you want it to be more luxy), stir well to warm it through and serve immediately with some fresh coriander scattered on top.

You could have some fresh bread with it to soak up all those lovely juices.

Venison Sausage & Mushroom Pasta

This is a guaranteed crowd pleaser and a fun way to use sausages for a quick supper. I tend to use rigatoni pasta, but any shape will work beautifully.

Serves 4 - 6

- 12-16 Venison sausages
- 2 tbsp olive oil
- 400g rigatoni pasta
- 250g mushrooms, finely sliced
- 1 red onion finely sliced
- 5 garlic cloves crushed
- 300g full fat crème fraiche
- Fresh parsley to garnish

Method:

1. Cut each sausage into 3 fat pieces.
2. Heat 1 tablespoon of olive oil in a deep frying pan and fry the sausages on the hot plate until brown all over then remove them and pop on a plate in the warming oven.
3. Cook the pasta according to the instructions.
4. Meanwhile, heat 1 tablespoon of olive oil in the frying pan and add in the onions, garlic and mushrooms. Fry gently on the simmering plate until they are all soft.
5. Add the sausages back into the pan and stir well.
6. Pop in the crème fraiche and stir.
7. Once the pasta is ready, drain it (reserving 2 tablespoons of the pasta water) and add it to the sausages. Mix well and add in some of the pasta water bit by bit until you have the sauce consistency you are looking for.
8. Garnish with the chopped fresh parsley.
9. Enjoy with garlic bread. Belissimo!

Venison Sausages with Juniper Berries and Red Current Gravy

This recipe is suited to cosy Winter nights with friends and a fire.

Serves 6

- 12-18 Venison sausages
- 2 tbsp olive oil
- 200g bacon lardons
- 2 large red onions, cut in half and finely sliced
- 4 garlic cloves, peeled and crushed
- 500ml beef stock
- 300 ml red wine
- 1 tbsp juniper berries, crushed with a pestle and mortar
- 1 tbsp redcurrant jelly
- Coriander to garnish

Method:

1. Heat 2 tablespoons of olive oil in a heavy based pan on the hot plate and once hot, brown the Venison sausages well all over then remove them to a plate and place in a warm oven.

2. Move the pan to the simmering plate, add the onions to the pan and fry until a golden colour then add the crushed garlic and cook for a few minutes. Now add the bacon lardons, move to the hot plate and fry until well coloured.

3. Pop in the beef stock and red wine, bring to a gentle bubble and cook until it reduces by half.

4. Add the Venison sausages back into the pan, add the crushed juniper berries and season.

5. Put a lid on the pan and place in the simmering oven of the Aga for around 30 minutes. Remove the lid, add in the redcurrant jelly, mix well and place the pan back in the oven for a further 20 minutes which should reduce and thicken the gravy.

6. Sprinkle with coriander and serve with lots of creamy mashed potatoes and some roasted parsnips.

Venison Sausage Pasta with Tomatoes and Spinach

Spicy and scrumptious, this recipe uses Lazy Chilli which I am an enormous fan of and always have a jar in the cupboard - it makes meal preparation so much easier than having to chop individual chillies.

Serves 4 - 6

- 12-16 Venison sausages each cut into 3 fat pieces
- 2 tbsp olive oil
- 1 onion diced finely
- 6 garlic cloves, peeled and crushed
- 1 tin chopped tomatoes
- 1 litre passata sauce
- 1 can sweetcorn
- 500ml chicken stock
- ½ tsp of Lazy Chilli (more if you like it spicy!)
- 400g dried pasta
- 1 bag fresh spinach
- 3 tbsp full fat creme fraiche
- 50g parmesan cheese, grated to garnish

Method:

1. Take a large pan with a tight fitting lid, add the olive oil and heat it up on the hot plate. Once hot, add the sausages and brown them all over until they are a good nutty brown colour.

2. Move the pan to the simmering plate, add the onions and garlic and cook for another 5 minutes. Then add the can of chopped tomatoes, passata, chicken stock, Lazy Chillies, sweetcorn and dried pasta. Stir well and cover with the lid. Allow it to boil then pop the pan in the baking oven of the Aga (or just let it simmer on the hob) for 15 minutes.

3. Now add the spinach to the pasta and mix well. Return it to the oven for a further 5 minutes (or until the pasta is cooked). Remove from the heat and stir in the creme fraiche one tablespoon at a time until it is thick and creamy. Season and top with the parmesan cheese.

4. Enjoy with a warming glass of red wine and relax knowing there is just one pan to wash up!

Walled Garden Sausages

We enjoy this recipe in the Autumn using apples from our walled garden. It is a hearty one pot meal which is sure to become one of your family's favourites too. I always make a large pot of it and freeze some for another night.

Serves 8

- 32 Venison sausages
- 4 tbsp olive oil
- 2 sweet potatoes, peeled and diced into $\frac{1}{4}$ inch pieces
- 2 apples, cored and sliced into chunks
- 2 red onions, halved and sliced into chunky rings
- 4 tbsp runny honey
- 2 tsp English mustard
- Fresh parsley to garnish

Method:

1. Take a large oven proof tray and pop in the sausages, sweet potato and onions. Drizzle over 3 tablespoons of olive oil and mix well so the food is evenly coated.

2. Pop the tray on the base of the roasting oven for 20 minutes.

3. Mix the honey and mustard together with a further tablespoon of olive oil.

4. After 20 minutes, remove the tray from the oven, add the apple then drizzle over the honey and mustard mixture ensuring the sausages, sweet potatoes, apple and onions are evenly coated.

5. Return the tray to the oven for a further 20 minutes then remove, sprinkle with the fresh parsley and serve.

Page 35

Page 36

Page 39

Page 43

Page 44

Page 47

Page 60

Page 64

Page 68

Casseroles

Here are some of my family's favourite casseroles incorporating many different flavours and all are super simple to make. Diced Venison casserole usually comes as a cut from the shoulder or haunch of the beastie. Remember the golden rule for casserole – cook it long and low and I promise it will be scrumptious. If you have a slow cooker, this chapter will work brilliantly.

Although there is nothing more comforting during the Winter months than a plate of warming casserole, this cut of Venison can be used throughout the year and instead of serving it with mashed potatoes, try salad, couscous or wild rice. It's particularly useful for those of us living in Scotland when we often need warmed up during Spring and Summer too!

My portion suggestion is just that, a suggestion, so if you are feeding a hungry bunch, do increase the amount of Venison used. Our family usually find 500g feeds the 4 of us with plenty of vegetables and sides however those with bigger appetites may wish to use more.

Catalonian Venison

This is such a versatile recipe – serve it with salad and crusty bread in the Summer or mashed potato for a cosy Winter supper.

For 8 people, you will need:

- 1kg Venison casserole
- 3 tbsp olive oil
- 2 red onions finely sliced
- 150g diced chorizo
- 6 garlic cloves, peeled and crushed
- 3 tsp smoked paprika
- 3 tsp oregano
- 2 tbsp tomato puree
- 2 orange peppers cut into 1 inch chunks
- 2 yellow peppers cut into 1 inch chunks
- 1 litre passata sauce
- 2 tins of butter beans, drained and rinsed
- 300ml beef stock
- Fresh herbs to garnish

Method:

1. Pop the olive oil in a heavy based pan, heat it up on the hot plate and once hot, move the pan to the simmering plate, add in the onions and garlic, cooking gently for 5 minutes stirring constantly.

2. Add the chorizo, and cook slowly for 5 minutes to allow the lovely red oils and flavours to escape to the onions and garlic.

3. Now brown the Venison in this pan (depending on the size of your pan you may need to do this in batches) ensuring it goes a lovely nutty brown colour.

4. Pop in the paprika, oregano and tomato puree. Mix well.

5. Now add in the peppers and give it all a good stir. Pop in the passata and stock, mixing all the time.

6. Once it is bubbling, leave it uncovered for 15 minutes then pop on the lid and put it in the simmering oven (or slow cooker) and leave it there for 5 hours.

7. Remove the pan from the simmering oven, add the drained butter beans, stir well and pop back in for a further 30 minutes.

8. Serve garnished with fresh herbs..

Venison Goulash

This is a wonderful way of feeding lots of people a very special dish which looks impressive and tastes delicious without spending hours slaving over a hot stove. Do remember that you may require more Venison depending on who you are feeding!

Serves 14 - 16

- 2kg Venison casserole
- 5 tbsp olive oil
- 2 large red onions finely diced
- 4 red or yellow peppers cut into chunks
- 4 garlic cloves finely sliced
- 2 tbsp flour plain
- 4 tsp hot paprika
- 4 tsp sweet paprika
- 4 tbsp tomato puree
- 1 litre beef stock
- 300ml sour cream

Method:

1. Heat 3 tablespoons of olive oil in a heavy based pan on the hot plate. Sear the Venison in batches then put on a warm plate and place in the plate warming oven of the Aga or a very low oven.

2. Add a further 2 tablespoons of oil into the pan and fry the onions for 10 minutes then move the pan to the simmering plate, add the peppers and garlic and fry, stirring constantly. Stir in the flour and spices. Cook for 3 minutes and then stir in the tomato puree and beef stock. Bring to a gentle simmer and add the Venison back in. Make sure the Venison is covered with the sauce and if not add in a little more beef stock and stir well.

3. Pop the lid on the pan and place it in the simmering oven for 5 hours.

4. When ready to serve, season, then swirl in the sour cream and scatter with fresh herbs – serve with parmentier potatoes or rice, a cheeky Rioja and lots of friends.

Piquant Pantry Venison Curry

Please don't be put off by the list of spices – they will all be lurking about your pantry. Although the list of ingredients is long, they are all readily accessible (I can even find them in rural Scotland!) and the methodology is simple. Like all spice dishes, this tastes even better the next day and it freezes well.

For 8 people, you will need:

- 1kg Venison casserole
- 2 tbsp vegetable oil
- 2 tsp mustard seeds
- 2 tsp fennel seeds
- 2 tsp cumin seeds
- 2 tsp ground ginger
- 4 red onions finely diced
- 8 garlic cloves, peeled and crushed
- 2 tsp Lazy Chilli
- 2 chicken stock cubes dissolved in 800ml of boiling water.
- Tub of natural yoghurt

For the Curry Seasoning:

- 2 tsp cumin seeds
- 2 tsp coriander seeds
- 2 tsp fennel seeds
- 1 tsp Lazy Chilli
- 1 tsp turmeric
- 1 tsp Bo Tree seasoning black peppercorns

Method:

1. Collect the curry seasoning ingredients and place to one side – we are going to deal with this part first. Take a non-stick frying pan and pop it on the simmering plate then add the cumin, coriander and fennel mixing lightly. Once you smell the delicious spices, add the remaining ingredients, mix well then remove from the heat. Transfer the spices to a pestle and mortar and grind well. Leave to the side for now.

2. Place a heavy based pan on the simmering plate, add in the vegetable oil and once hot, add the mustard seeds, fennel and cumin then cook with the lid on for 3-4 minutes.

3. Now add the onions and cook gently until soft, stirring well then add the garlic, ginger and chilli. Cook for 4-5 minutes then add the Venison and brown well – depending on the size of your pan you may need to do this in batches.

4. Sprinkle over the curry seasoning mixture and mix so the Venison is well coated. Add the hot stock so it covers the meat and allow to bubble gently.

5. Reduce the heat and pop in the simmering oven for 3 hours. After this time, take out the Venison, mix well and add more stock if necessary and pop back in for a further 2 hours. If the sauce needs thickened, pop the pan on the hot plate and boil rapidly.

6. Garnish with coriander and a good dollop of natural yoghurt.

7. Serve with rice and poppadoms.

Italian Venison Casserole

This is an easy, one pot alternative to traditional Italian tomato sauce which is delicious with pasta yet equally scrumptious with mashed potato or couscous.

Serves 10 - 12

- 1.5kg casserole
- 2 tbsp olive oil
- 75g plain flour
- 100g pancetta
- 3 carrots finely diced
- 2 celery sticks finely diced
- 1 onion finely diced
- 6 garlic cloves, peeled and crushed
- 250ml dry white wine
- 400g passata sauce
- 400ml beef stock
- 1 tsp rosemary
- 1 tsp sage
- 2 tbsp capers rinsed and drained
- Fresh parsley

Method:

1. Season the flour and mix the Venison through ensuring it is covered evenly.

2. Heat the olive oil in a heavy based pan on the hot plate and brown the Venison in batches to ensure each piece is a lovely deep brown colour. Remove to a warm plate.

3. Move the pan to the simmering plate, add the pancetta to the pan with the carrot, celery, onion and garlic and cook gently for 5 minutes.

4. Now return the Venison to the pan. Stir in the wine, stock, passata and herbs.

5. Pop on the lid, bring to the boil and simmer for 5 hours in the simmering oven.

6. Once ready to eat, stir through the capers and serve.

Fruity Sweet Curry

This is a very gentle curry which is loved by adults and children alike due to the sweetness of the fruit and the potatoes. You don't necessarily need to serve any further veg with it but we do love roasted broccoli and it adds a good splash of colour to the plate. This is a super simple recipe so get the children involved!

For 4 people, you will need:

- 500g Venison casserole
- 1 tbsp olive oil
- 2 shallots finely diced
- 1 large sweet potato, peeled and cut into 1 inch size cubes
- 1 can of full fat coconut milk
- 3 tbsp of Patak's Medium Spice Paste
- 2 tins of peaches, drained
- 4 spring onions finely sliced
- 2 tbsp of full fat creme fraiche

Method:

1. Pop the olive oil in the bottom of a heavy based pan, heat gently on the simmering plate then once hot, add the shallots and gently soften on the simmering plate.

2. Add the Venison and the curry paste, mix well then move to the hot plate allowing it to brown.

3. Pop in the sweet potato and coconut milk then mix well and bring it to a gentle simmer. Cover with a tight lid and place in the simmering oven for 5 hours.

4. Remove from the oven and add in the drained fruit (not the fruit juice!), mix well and pop back in the simmering oven for a further 30 minutes.

5. Remove from the oven, stir through the creme fraiche then mix in the spring onions, holding a handful back to scatter on top when serving.

Scrumptious Tagine

Quite simply, this is scrumptious. It is aromatic and warming so perfect for a cosy supper as the nights draw in. Don't be put off with the long list of store cupboard ingredients – it is super simple and perfect for freezing. We love this with either couscous or wild rice.

Serves 6 - 8

- 1kg Venison casserole
- 3 tbsp olive oil
- 2 red onions finely diced
- 2 tsp cayenne pepper
- 3 tsp ground black pepper
- 3 tsp paprika
- 3 tsp ground ginger
- 2 tsp turmeric
- 4 tsp ground cinnamon
- 6 garlic cloves, peeled and crushed
- 2 cans chopped tomatoes
- 1 handful dried apricots halved
- 1 handful sultanas
- 1 handful dried prunes halved
- 800ml beef stock
- 2 tbsp runny honey
- Fresh herbs to garnish

Method:

1. Mix the cayenne pepper, black pepper, paprika, ginger, turmeric and cinnamon together. This is your spice mix.

2. Place the Venison casserole meat in a bowl and cover with half the spice mix. Leave it to marinade for as long as possible.

3. Heat the olive oil in a heavy based pan on the simmering plate, add the onions and gently fry for 10 minutes until they are soft and translucent. Then add the rest of the spice mix, the garlic and gently cook for a further 5 minutes.

4. Now add in the Venison and brown it on all sides so it is a lovely deep brown colour. Depending on the size of your pan you may need to do this in batches.

5. Pop in the tins of tomatoes together with the honey, stock and dried fruit. Combine well, allow it to bubble then put the lid on and place in the simmering oven for 6 hours until the meat is falling apart.

6. Enjoy with friends, a lovely glass of red and a roaring fire.

Colourful Casserole

This particular recipe, although wonderful in Winter, can also see us through a Scottish Spring and Summer when nights can be a bit chilly. We love this casserole with broccoli and cauliflower cheese.

Serves 4

- 500g Venison casserole
- 2 tbsp olive oil
- 1 red onion, finely diced
- 2 garlic cloves, peeled and crushed
- 2 red peppers cut into 1 inch size chunks
- 1 orange pepper cut into 1 inch size chunks
- 1 Oxo cube
- 500ml beef stock

Method:

1. Put the olive oil in a heavy based pan which has a tight-fitting lid and pop it on the simmering plate. Once it is hot, add the onions and garlic and fry gently until translucent.

2. Move the pan to the hot plate, add the Venison chunks and brown rapidly.

3. Crumble in the Oxo cube, mix it with the Venison and then add the chopped peppers.

4. Mix well and add in the stock.

5. Allow it all to bubble then pop on the lid and place in the simmering oven for 5 hours. Voila!

Pitscandly Venison Casserole

This is a zingy dish which I serve with roasted new potatoes and peas.

Serves 8

- 1kg Venison casserole
- 2 tbsp olive oil
- 1 tbsp of butter
- 4 cloves garlic finely sliced
- 1 tbsp plain flour
- 3 red onions finely sliced
- 800 ml beef stock
- 2 Oxo cubes
- 3 tangerines
- Fresh parsley to garnish

Method:

1. Melt the butter and olive oil in a large heavy based pan on the simmering plate.
2. Whilst this is happening, dust the Venison with the flour until the pieces are evenly coated.
3. Once the butter has melted, brown the meat on all sides until it becomes a rich brown colour. This may need to be done in batches.
4. Once the meat is browned, crumble over the Oxo cubes and mix well. Remove the Venison with a slotted spoon and keep it on a plate in the warming oven.
5. Finely slice the onions and fry them gently in the pan with the remainder of the oil and butter from browning the meat. Add in the thinly sliced garlic and fry gently for 5 minutes not allowing the mixture to stick. Use the simmering plate.
6. Grate the rind from each tangerine then half them and squeeze the juice from each and quarter the skins.
7. Once the onions have softened return the Venison to the pan and add in the orange juice together with the quartered skins.
8. Stir everything well – the smells are amazing.
9. Add in the beef stock, bring to the boil, scatter over the rind, pop on the lid and place in the simmering oven for 5 hours.
10. Check the Venison half way through, stir and add more stock if necessary.
11. Serve garnished with fresh parsley.

Venison with Beer and Butterbeans

Although you must plan ahead with this recipe, it is worth it and the process is simple. I have been known to cook this in the slow oven overnight – the long and low golden rule certainly applies and you will all love it.

For 4 people, you will need:

- 500g Venison casserole
- 2 tbsp olive oil
- 6 garlic cloves peeled and crushed
- 1 tbsp soft brown sugar
- 1 tbsp Dijon mustard
- 1 tsp black pepper
- 1 tsp cumin
- 2 tsp paprika
- 4 red onions finely sliced
- 500ml dark beer or ale
- 1 can butterbeans, drained and rinsed

Method:

1. Take a large container which has a lid and pop in the garlic, sugar, mustard, 1 tbsp olive oil, pepper, cumin, paprika, then add the Venison and mix well to ensure it is evenly coated.

2. Marinade for 24 hours if possible.

3. When ready to cook, ensure the meat is at room temperature then take a heavy bottomed pan with a tight-fitting lid and pop in 1 tbsp olive oil. Place the pan on the simmering plate and once hot, add the onions and fry gently until soft.

4. Move the pan to the hot plate, add the Venison (and its marinade) browning it fast, then add the butterbeans and beer, mix well and replace the lid.

5. Once it is bubbling, remove it from the hot plate and pop it in the simmering oven for 5 hours. Enjoy!

Venison with Apricots and Raisins

This is a perfect pantry recipe which can come to your rescue when inspiration is needed.

Serves 4

- 500g Venison casserole
- 1 tbsp olive oil
- 1 tbsp butter
- 1 red onion finely diced
- 300ml red wine
- 300ml apple juice
- 1 tsp ground cinnamon
- 30g raisins
- 30g dried apricots halved
- 1 tsp ground ginger

Method:

1. Mix together the wine, apple juice, raisins, apricots, cinnamon and ginger then pour over the Venison and marinade overnight.

2. When you are ready to cook, remove the Venison from the fridge and ensure it is at room temperature before you start cooking.

3. Take a heavy based pan with a tight-fitting lid and pop in the butter and olive oil and heat this rapidly on the hot plate.

4. Take the Venison chunks out of the marinade and brown them on all sides until they are a deep nutty brown then add the onions. Move the pan to the simmering plate and fry gently.

5. Add the marinade back into the pan, bring to the boil and then place in the simmering oven for 5 hours.

6. Enjoy with cous cous, Rosé wine and plenty of chatter.

Venison, Chorizo and Cider "Pie"

As Venison is such a healthy meat I don't like smothering it in pastry so this is my "pie" cheat! I simply cook the filling as a normal casserole then cut out a pastry shape, usually a circle or a heart, and pop it on top just before serving.

Serves 8

- 1kg Venison casserole
- 2 tbsp of olive oil
- 1 onion, finely diced
- 2 leeks trimmed and finely sliced
- 200g chorizo cut into small cubes
- 2 carrots finely chopped
- 2 celery sticks finely sliced
- 2 tbsp plain flour
- 500ml cider
- 4 tbsp full fat crème fraiche
- 1 tbsp wholegrain mustard
- 1 pack puff pastry
- 1 egg, cracked and whisked well to make egg wash

Method:

1. Heat the olive oil in a heavy based pan on the simmering plate. Add the onion, leeks and chorizo and gently cook until the leeks and onion soften and you see the lovely oils coming out of the chorizo.

2. Transfer the pan to the hot plate, add the Venison and stir well, browning the meat.

3. After 5 minutes mix in the flour, add the celery and carrots then pour in the cider and bring to the boil.

4. Once bubbling, move the pan to the simmering plate and stir in the mustard then put on the lid and pop in the simmering oven for 5 hours. You can stir it occasionally if you wish.

5. After this time, stir in the crème fraiche and return to the simmering oven for a further 30 minutes.

6. Meanwhile, take your ready made puff pastry, roll it out and cut out the number of shapes you require, brush with some egg wash and cook the pastry according to the packet instructions.

7. When ready to eat, pop some casserole on a plate and top with the cooked pastry shape and voila, a wonderful "pie" without too much bulky, unhealthy pastry.

Leek & Tarragon Venison

This is a scrumptious one pot Venison recipe which is flexible as sometimes I have substituted leeks with left over Brussel Sprouts and peas instead of green beans - just use what you have in your fridge.

Serves 4

- 500g of Venison casserole
- 1 tbsp olive oil
- 2 tsp heaped plain flour
- 1 onion finely diced
- 2 large leeks chopped into thick slices
- 500ml chicken stock
- 150ml full fat crème fraiche
- 7 tsp Dijon mustard
- 4 garlic cloves, peeled and crushed
- 7 tsp dried tarragon
- 200g trimmed green beans (or peas if you have them handy)
- Fresh parsley to garnish

Method:

1. Get a heavy based pan with a tight-fitting lid. Pop in the olive oil, place on the simmering plate and once hot, add the onions and garlic and fry gently. Add in the Venison chunks, flour and brown all over mixing really well.

2. Add in the leeks and stock, mix well until it bubbles then bang on the lid and pop it in the simmering oven for 4 hours.

3. Remove the pan from the oven, pop on the simmering plate and add in the green beans (or peas).

4. In a bowl whisk together the crème fraiche, mustard and tarragon then add it to the pan.

5. Mix well and pop back in the simmering oven for an hour.

6. To serve, sprinkle with parsley and enjoy it with some fresh crusty bread to soak up all those scrummy juices. If you are trying to get more veg into children then I recommend roasting some sweet potato and red onions and having it on a plate all together. It also goes really well with pasta.

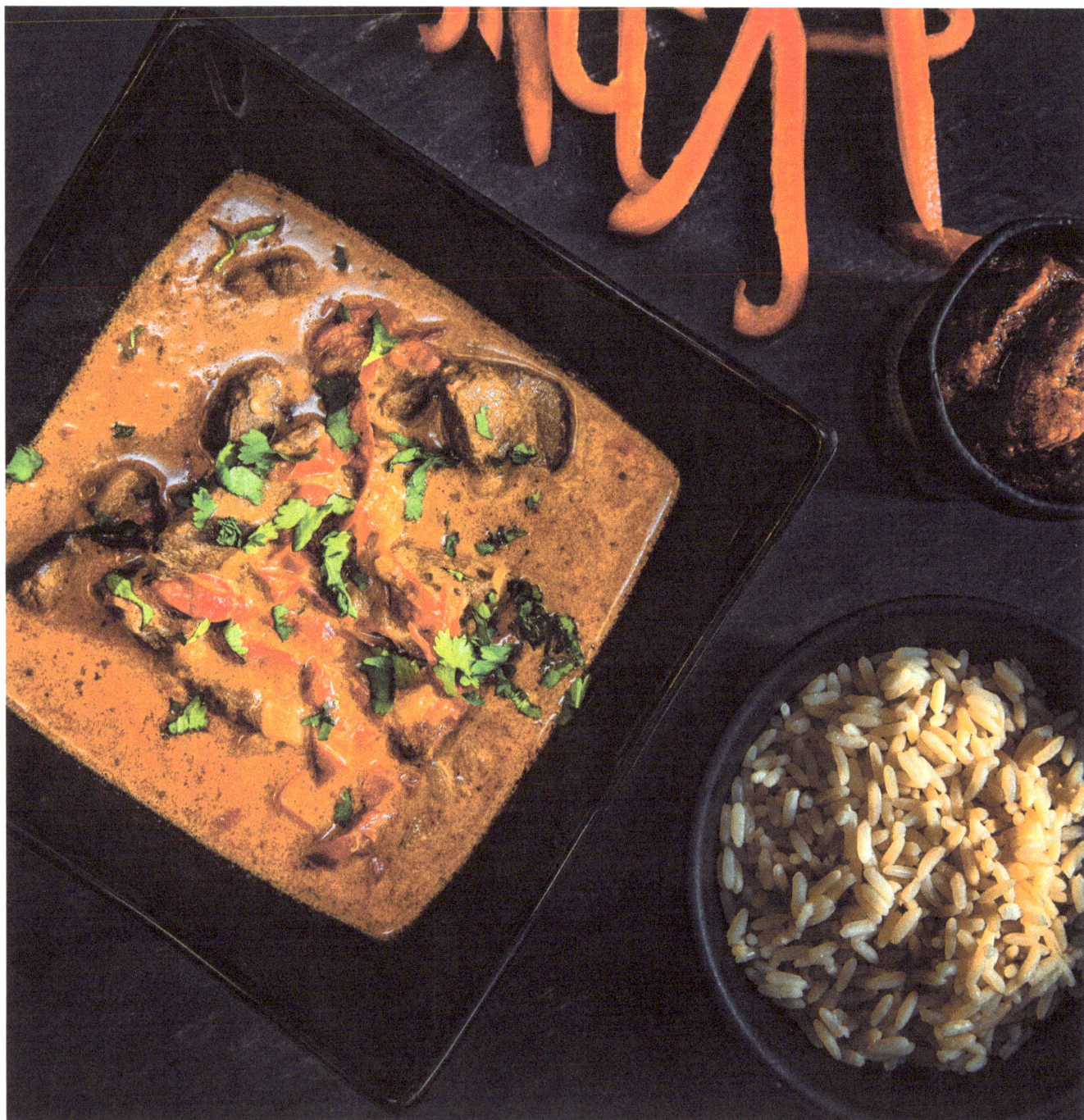

Venison Thai Curry

This is another simply scrumptious one pot recipe which freezes perfectly so I usually double the ingredients and freeze half for a future emergency supper.

Serves 4

- 500g diced Venison casserole
- 1 tbsp olive oil
- 2 garlic cloves, peeled and crushed
- 1 red onion halved and finely sliced
- 2 red peppers finely sliced longways
- 1 jar of Thai red curry paste
- 1 can full fat coconut milk
- Fresh coriander to serve

Method:

1. Take a heavy bottomed pan (which has a tight-fitting lid), pop in the olive oil and put it on the simmering plate.

2. When it is hot add the onions and garlic and gently soften.

3. Add in the Venison and brown well until it is a deep nutty brown.

4. Pop in the finely sliced peppers and mix them through the Venison.

5. Now add the jar of curry paste, mix well then add in the coconut milk and gently stir.

6. Once it bubbles, pop the lid on and place in the simmering oven for 5 hours.

7. Serve with sticky rice and a big smile knowing there is hardly any washing up to do!

Harissa Venison with Crispy Potatoes

This is a really delicious, easy supper, which I like to serve on a large platter in the middle of the table so everyone can dive in. I use a smoked Harissa paste with chilli but any Harissa will work.

For 4 people, you will need:

- 500g Venison casserole
- 4 tbsp olive oil
- 600g potatoes cut into 1 inch chunks
- 2 red onions halved then cut into wedges
- 1 small white onion finely diced
- 400g of tinned chopped tomatoes (or passata sauce)
- 150ml cold water
- 4 tsp Harissa paste
- 1 tsp garlic puree
- 2 tsp dried oregano
- 200g feta cheese, crumbled
- 3 tbsp chopped fresh parsley
- 2 tbsp chopped fresh mint
- 2 tbsp chopped fresh coriander

Method:

1. Pop 2 tablespoons of olive oil in a heavy based pan (which has a lid), heat on the hot plate and add the garlic puree, finely diced white onion and soften gently on the simmering plate.

2. Move the pan to the hot plate, add the Venison and brown fast then mix in the Harissa paste so all the meat is well coated.

3. Add the can of tomatoes (or passata sauce) and then add the cold water to the empty tin or jar of tomatoes and swill around, getting all the last bits of tomato and add that to the pan too.

4. Stir well, bring to the boil, put on the lid and pop the pan in the simmering oven for 5 hours.

5. Meanehile put two tablespoons of olive oil in an oven proof deep roasting dish and heat it up for a few minutes in the roasting oven then add your potato chunks and red onions, coat well in the oil and season then roast for 40 minutes in the roasting oven. Once cooked, transfer to the simmering oven to keep them warm.

6. Once the meat is cooked, remove the potato dish from the simmering oven and spoon over the hot Venison and all the delicious sauce.

7. Finally, crumble the Feta cheese over the top then pop into the hot roasting oven for 15 minutes.

8. After this time, remove it, scatter over the herbs and serve immediately.

Tasty Venison "Pie"

This is another crowd pleaser and if you are watching your calories the good news is it isn't smothered in pastry.

Serves 6 - 8

- 1kg of Venison casserole
- 3 tbsp olive oil
- 1 tbsp of butter
- 2 red onions finely diced
- 1 tbsp plain flour
- 2 tsp English mustard powder
- 5 carrots, diced
- 500ml dark ale or stout
- 1 tbsp brown sugar
- 4 ginger biscuits grated or bashed in a bag
- 1 packet ready made puff pastry

Method:

1. Heat half the butter and 2 tablespoons of olive oil in a heavy based pan on the hot plate, brown the Venison then remove it from the pan to a warmed plate and set aside. Depending on the size of your pan you may need to do this in batches.

2. Heat the rest of the butter and olive oil on the simmering plate and add in the onions mixing until soft. Remove from the heat and stir in the flour and mustard powder and stir until it is a thick mix.

3. Add back the Venison and the diced carrots and mix well.

4. Pour in the dark ale (or stout), brown sugar, vinegar and grated (or bashed down in a bag) ginger biscuits and stir well.

5. Put on a tight fitting lid and once it is simmering, pop it in the simmering oven for 5 hours.

6. After this time, remove from the oven, stir well, replace and cook for a further hour. Add more ale or stout if necessary

7. Cut the ready made pastry into desired shapes (I like circles or hearts) with cookie cutters and cook according to the packet instructions.

8. Serve the venison on a plate with peas and top with the pastry - a deconstructed, delicious non "pie", "pie"!! Enjoy!

Friday Night Curry

This is a firm favourite with us – scrumptious every time and not much washing up!

For 4 people, you will need:

- 500g Venison casserole
- 1 tbsp olive oil
- 1 red onion finely diced
- 3 garlic cloves crushed
- 1 courgette diced
- 400g can chopped tomatoes
- 3 tbsp Tikka curry paste
- 2 tbsp tomato puree
- 3 tbsp mango chutney
- 8 cherry tomatoes halved
- 1 tbsp full fat crème fraiche
- Handful of fresh coriander

Method:

1. Take a large, heavy based pan with a lid, add in the tablespoon of olive oil and heat it up on the hot plate. Once hot, add the Venison, brown it well then transfer the pan to the simmering plate.

2. Now add the onion and garlic then fry gently for 5 minutes.

3. Add the rest of the ingredients (apart from the crème fraiche) and mix well.

4. Bring to the boil, put on the lid tightly then pop in the simmering oven for 5 hours.

5. Remove the pan, stir through the crème fraiche and pop back in the simmering oven for a further hour.

6. When ready to serve, top with the fresh coriander and serve with lots of comforting rice – happy Friday!

Venison with Chocolate and Chilli

This is a real dinner party show stopper – it is simple to make but retains the wow factor so you can bask in the glory of adulation from your friends without too much cooking stress.

For 8 people, you will need:

- 1kg Venison casserole
- 3 tbsp olive oil
- 1 tbsp plain flour
- 2 red onions finely diced
- 4 garlic cloves, peeled and crushed
- 1 tsp Lazy Chilli
- 800ml beef stock
- 9 squares of good quality dark chocolate

Method:

1. Pop the flour in a bowl and add in the Venison casserole chunks ensuring they are evenly coated.

2. Heat the olive oil in a heavy based pan and brown the Venison well. Unless your pan is enormous you will need to do this in batches to ensure the chunks all turn a lovely nutty brown.

3. Once browned, place the meat on a warmed dish and pop in the plate warming oven of the Aga.

4. Add the onions and garlic to the heavy based pan and sauté for 5 minutes on the simmering plate.

5. Stir in the Lazy Chilli, stock and stir well. Add the venison back in, bring to the boil and add 4 squares of the grated dark chocolate into the pan and stir well.

6. Pop on the lid and place it in the baking oven for 1 hour.

7. After that time, remove the pan, stir the contents well and add in the further 5 squares of grated chocolate stirring well to ensure the sauce is glossy. Add more stock if necessary, put the lid back on and place in the simmering oven for 5 hours.

8. Serve with lashings of mashed potatoes and roasted beetroot.

Spicy Ginger Venison

As with all spicy dishes, this tastes even better the next day so do make it ahead of schedule if you can.

For 4 people, you will need:

- 500g Venison casserole
- 4 tbsp vegetable oil
- 2 large orange peppers cut into 1 inch size chunks
- 1 red onion, finely diced
- 1 tbsp butter
- 2 tbsp garlic puree
- 1 tbsp ground ginger
- 1 tsp Himalayan salt
- 1 heaped tsp Lazy Chilli
- 1 tablespoon of tomato puree
- 1 tbsp medium curry powder
- 2 tbsp garam masala
- 1 tsp ground cinnamon
- 1 tin kidney beans (drained and rinsed)
- 300ml of chicken stock

Method:

1. Pop the butter and oil into a large heavy based pan with a lid and let it heat gently on the simmering plate.

2. Once hot and the butter melted, add the garlic puree, ginger, onions and salt then fry gently until the onions are a soft and translucent.

3. Add the Lazy Chilli, tomato puree, curry powder, garam masala, cinnamon and mix together. Cook for around 10 minutes to release the aromas.

4. Move the pan to the hot plate, add the Venison and mix it all together, ensuring it is brown all over. Depending on the size of the pan, you may have to do this in batches.

5. Drain the can of kidney beans and give them a quick rinse with cold water. Chop the large coloured peppers into roughly 1 inch size chunks.

6. Add the kidney beans and the peppers to the pan with the Venison, give it all a good stir, add in the chicken stock and make sure it is bubbling. Pop it in the baking oven for 1 hour then move to the simmering oven for 5 hours.

7. I like to serve this with sticky rice and smashed avocado. I then drizzle some single cream or creme fraiche over the top when it has been plated up. A scattering of fresh parsley or coriander would finish it off beautifully.

Page 73

Page 74

Page 77

Page 81

Shanks

These are such an underrated cut of Venison – do ask your butcher or local supplier for them and remember they are budget friendly as I find one shank will generally feed our family of 4 as they are rich and can be served with lots of side dishes. However if you are cooking for hungry adults you may need to use another shank. Remember the golden rules; shanks need cooked long and low.

Shanks are perfect to cook in your slow cooker making them a wonderful one pot meal which you can pop on to cook in the morning and know it will be ready and scrumptious for you at supper time. I always suggest cooking shanks for as long as possible – I have been known to leave them overnight in the plate warming oven of the Aga, but do always ensure there is lots of delicious sauce so they remain moist.

I have included some cosy kitchen supper recipes the family will love such as Ragu which is wonderful with pasta, and also some more sophisticated recipes with intense, rich flavours for adult palates.

With all these recipes, you need a large heavy based pan which has a tight-fitting lid or do use your slow cooker.

Happily these are one pot recipes which keep things simple, and of course, always scrumptious.

Venison Shanks with Garlic

This recipe oozes with flavour. I love this with lashings of mashed potato and peas.

Serves 4

- 1 Venison shank
- 1 tbsp olive oil
- 1 tbsp butter
- 4 garlic bulbs, peeled
- 4 onions finely diced
- 400ml white wine
- 400ml chicken stock
- 200ml double cream
- 1 tsp dried thyme
- 1 tsp dried chives
- Zest of one lemon

Method:

1. Heat the olive oil and butter in a heavy based pan on the hotplate and brown the shank well all over then remove from the pan and place on a warmed plate. Transfer the pan to the simmering plate.

2. Add the onions and garlic to the heavy based pan with the lovely venison shank juices and gently cook for 5 minutes on the simmering plate. Pour in the wine, stock, herbs, lemon zest and bring to the boil gently.

3. Return the shank to the pot, cover with a tight-fitting lid and cook in the baking oven for an hour. Remove, turn the shank over and add further hot stock if necessary. Transfer the pan to the simmering oven (or slow cooker) for 5 hours.

4. Remove the pan from the oven and take out a few of the best garlic cloves for decoration.

5. Remove the shank and puree the sauce with a hand blender, pour in the cream gently stirring it through and allow it to heat slowly. Leave on a gentle heat.

6. Using 2 forks remove the meat from the shank and add the meat back into the pan with the sauce and mix it all well. Discard any sinew.

7. Garnish with the whole cloves of garlic and serve.

Venison Shanks with Redcurrents

This is a great recipe to use up fruit from the garden. I usually have an abundance of frozen redcurrants in the freezer and simply defreeze them the night before. As this recipe can be frozen, I have doubled it so you can pop half in the freezer – it will taste even more delicious the next time!

Serves 8

- 2 Venison shanks
- 3 tbsp olive oil
- 1 tbsp butter
- 4 red onions finely diced
- 2 celery stalks chopped into 1cm pieces
- 2 punnets of redcurrants / 227g jar of redcurrant jelly
- 400ml red wine
- 400ml beef stock
- 2 tsp juniper berries

Method:

1. Crush the juniper berries in a pestle and mortar and scatter over the shanks rubbing in well.
2. Heat the butter and 2 tablespoons of olive oil in a heavy based pan on the hot plate.
3. When the pan is hot brown the shanks on all sides then remove them to a warm plate.
4. Add another tablespoon of oil to the pan then pop in the onions and celery and gently soften on the simmering plate.
5. Add the redcurrants (or the jar of jelly) and simmer. Return the shanks to the pan, add the stock and wine then stir until gently bubbling.
6. Put the lid on and place the pan in the baking oven for 1 hour then transfer to the simmering oven for a minimum of 5 hours until the Venison is falling off the bone.
7. Remove the shanks from the pan and pull the meat off the bone with 2 forks, discarding all the sinew. Now, boil up the sauce until it is thick and glossy.
8. Return the shredded meat to the glossy sauce, mix well and serve with roast potatoes and your favourite veggies – yum.

Venison Shanks with Red Wine and Balsamic

This is a really simple recipe as it uses store cupboard ingredients so it's a case of raiding the larder and popping it all in the slow cooker – perfect!

Serves 4

- 1 Venison shank
- 1 tbsp olive oil
- 600ml beef stock
- 300ml red wine
- 6 tbsp balsamic vinegar
- 3 tbsp tomato puree
- 5 crushed garlic cloves
- 1 tsp lemon zest or 1 tbsp of lemon juice from a bottle

Method:

1. Mix together the stock, wine, balsamic vinegar, tomato puree, garlic and lemon zest. Place this aside for now.

2. Heat the oil in a heavy bottomed pan on the hot plate and when hot brown the shank on all sides.

3. Now pour the mixture over the shanks.

4. Cover with a tightly fitting lid and once bubbling, transfer it to the baking oven for 1 hour then turn the shank over and transfer to the simmering oven for a further 5 hours until the meat is falling off the bone. I prefer using the plate warming oven of the Aga overnight.

5. Use 2 forks to pull the meat off the bone and ensure any sinew is discarded.

6. Serve with roast potatoes and roast beetroot.

Rosé Shanks

Usually shanks recipes are quite wintery so I wanted to create a summery recipe and what better wine to use than a delicious pink Rosé! Make sure you enjoy a glass while cooking.

Serves 4

- 1 Venison shank
- 1 tbsp olive oil
- 1 tbsp butter
- 6 shallots finely sliced
- 4 garlic bulbs with each clove peeled but keep them whole
- 500 ml Rosé wine
- 400 ml chicken stock
- 2 tsp of dried thyme
- 2 tsp of dried rosemary
- Zest of 2 lemons

Method:

1. Heat the olive oil and butter in a heavy based pan (which has a tight-fitting lid) and brown the shank well on all sides on the hot plate then remove it and set it aside meantime.

2. Transfer the pan to the simmering plate and add the shallots and garlic. Gently cook in the lovely juices for 5 or 6 minutes.

3. Add the wine and mix well then add the stock, dried herbs and the zest of one lemon. Mix well.

4. Return the shank to the pot, place the lid on firmly and cook in the baking oven for an hour. After that time remove it, turn the shank over then transfer to the simmering oven for 5 hours so the meat is falling off the bone.

5. Once it is cooked, remove the pan from the oven and take out the shank. Blitz the sauce with a hand blender so it is thick and creamy.

6. Use two forks to shred the Venison then return the meat to the pan with the blitzed sauce, scatter over the zest of the second lemon and serve immediately with salad and peas or brown rice and roasted peppers. YUM!

Scrumptious Ragu

This is simply the most comforting pasta feast you can imagine – it is an enormous hug in a bowl. I have doubled the recipe so you can pop half in the freezer for another time. The zesty topping makes it like an Osso Bucco so is fancy enough to be served to friends for supper.

Serves 8

- 2 Venison shanks
- 3 tbsp olive oil
- 1 tbsp butter
- 2 jars passata sauce
- 1 can chopped tomatoes
- 225g chorizo sausage, diced
- 2 tbsp dried Italian mixed herbs
- 1 large can sweetcorn, drained and rinsed
- 2 red onions, finely diced
- 5 cloves of garlic, crushed
- 1 leek finely diced
- 2 carrots finely diced
- 1 Oxo cube, crumbled
- 300 ml red wine
- Zest of 2 lemons
- 2 handfuls of fresh parsley finely chopped

Method:

1. Take your large heavy based pan and pop in 2 tablespoons of olive oil with the butter and heat on the hot plate. Once sizzling, brown the shanks on all sides then remove to a warm plate and pop to the side or in the plate warming oven.

2. Put another tablespoon of olive oil into the pan, and move it to the simmering plate, reducing the heat. Add in the chorizo, onions, leeks and garlic and gently soften, scraping up all the delicious bits from the bottom of the pan. Scatter over the crumbled Oxo cube and mix well.

3. Once these have softened add in the sweetcorn, carrots and Italian seasoning, then return the shanks to the pan.

4. Pour over the red wine, passata sauces and the can of chopped tomatoes and gently mix.

5. Pop the lid on tightly, bring to a gentle bubble then put the pan in the baking oven for an hour then transfer to the simmering oven for 5 hours. Half way through, turn the shanks over.

6. Once cooked and the meat is falling off the bone, remove the shanks from the pan and using two forks pull the meat apart into chunks returning it to the delicious sauce. Discard all the sinew.

7. Grate the 2 lemons over the top of the sauce then cover with the fresh parsley for a real punchy zing.

8. Serve with pasta, garlic bread and salad.

Page 84

Page 87

Page 88

Page 90

Page 92

Page 99

Page 102

Page 105

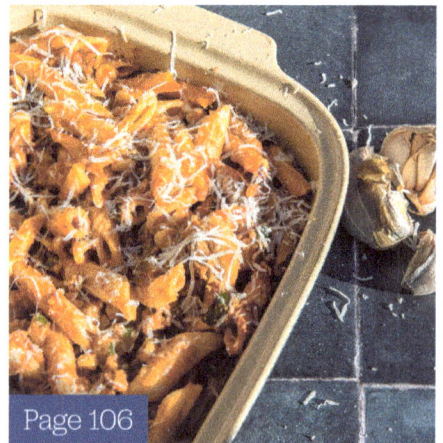
Page 106

Steak & Minute Steaks

As with Venison fillet, Venison steaks are incredibly lean with no thick border of fat so our golden rule for cooking these is: less is more. Generally steaks come from the haunch of the beastie and these recipes are for traditional thicker steaks and also thinner Minute Steaks.

Minute Steaks literally just need seconds in a hot pan whereas the thicker traditional steaks usually require a minute and a half on each side for rare.As it is so easy to over cook Venison, do have your stop watch at the ready and remember to rest the meat for at least 5 minutes before serving as the meat will continue to cook.

Venison steaks are fabulous on the barbecue too so do look at that chapter for more cooking inspiration.

As always, ensure the Venison is at room temperature before you start cooking.

Pitscandly Steaks

Venison steaks are a super treat to enjoy at the weekend as they are so quick and easy to cook – perfect with salads in the Summer or traditional potatoes and vegetables in the Winter.

You can of course do these steaks on the BBQ and they would be even more scrumptious with that delicious BBQ smokiness. The timings will be the same.

For perfect steaks you will need, for 2 people:

- 2 Venison haunch steaks
- 1 tbsp olive oil
- 1 tbsp Bo Tree White Pipali pepper Pearls
- 1 tbsp Bo Tree Herb de Kampot

Method:

1. Drizzle the olive oil onto a large plate then add the pepper and herbs and mix it all together.
2. Pop the steaks on the plate and rub the oil mixture well over both sides, turning the steaks over to ensure even coverage.
3. Leave in the fridge to marinade for at least an hour.
4. The steaks must be at room temperature before cooking so ensure you remove the venison from the fridge in good time.
5. Take a heavy griddle pan and pop it on the hot plate. Once it feels hot hot hot, add the steaks and leave for 90 seconds. They should make a wonderful sizzling sound when they hit the pan. Don't be tempted to move them around as you want the stripes from the pan.
6. After 90 seconds, turn the steaks over and leave them in the pan for a further 90 seconds.
7. Once the time is up, remove the pan from the heat and place the steaks on a board.
8. Leave to rest for 5 minutes then serve.

Scottish Stroganoff

OK, I admit this isn't the healthiest recipe but it is scrumptious and a really fabulous kitchen supper for friends. It is versatile as you can use Fillet, Minute Steaks or Steaks. Pop it on a big platter in the middle of the table and everyone can dig in!

For 4 people, you will need:

- 600g Venison Minute Steaks
- 2 tbsp olive oil
- 200g mushrooms finely sliced
- 2 red onions halved and finely sliced
- 200ml white wine
- 200ml beef stock
- 2 tbsp whiskey
- 200ml double cream
- Fresh coriander to garnish

Method:

1. Put 1 tablespoon of oil in a heavy based metal frying pan on the simmering plate and add the onions, cooking gently until soft.

2. Add the sliced mushrooms and again gently cook until soft on the simmering plate.

3. Add the wine and stir well, then add the stock, transfer to the hot plate and boil until the liquid is reduced by half.

4. Remove the mixture from the pan and place it in a pre-heated bowl and pop in the simmering oven.

5. Take your heavy based pan and pop in 1 tablespoon of olive oil, place on the hot plate and once hot add the Venison minute steaks. Cook them on each side for 30 seconds.

6. Remove the meat and place on a board to rest.

7. Again using the hot pan, add in the whiskey to the cooking juices and light it. Once the flames are out, add in the mixture from the simmering oven and stir well. Add in the cream and gently bring to the boil on the simmering plate.

8. Cut the meat into fingers size strips, add to the pan and mix well.

9. Take a large platter, pop wild rice on the bottom, top with the mixture and garnish with fresh coriander. Serve with green salad, a large spoon, red wine and friends.

Venison Minute Steaks with Oyster Sauce

This is a very jolly dish which is perfect to enjoy on Valentines Night! You do need to plan ahead though as the Venison steaks need to marinade so if you can, marinade them in the morning then leave in the fridge until Supper time.

For a romantic meal for 2 you will need:

- 300g Venison Minute Steaks
- 1 tbsp olive oil
- 1cm fresh ginger finely chopped
- 2 spring onions
- 200g green beans or long stemmed broccoli finely sliced
- 1 tbsp light soy sauce
- 3 tbsp fish sauce
- 1 tbsp cornflower
- 1 tsp brown sugar
- 1 tsp black pepper
- 3 tbsp oyster sauce
- 150ml chicken stock
- 1 lime - to squeeze the juice over the dish at the end
- a handful of spring onions and finely chopped dill to serve

Method:

1. Slice the Venison Minute Steaks into finger size strips, place in a bowl and add the soy sauce and fish sauce. Mix well then sprinkle over half the cornflower, mix well again and leave to marinade for at least 3 hours.

2. When you are ready to start cooking, blanch the broccoli or green beans in boiling water for 2-4 mins then drain and set aside.

3. Mix together the brown sugar, black pepper, oyster sauce, the remaining half of the corn flour and chicken stock then set aside. Pour a lovely glass of Rosé and have a slurp.

4. Heat a large non stick frying pan or wok and once very very hot, pan fry the Venison for no longer than a minute ensure it is brown on all sides. Remove the Venison and pop in a bowl and place in the Aga warming oven.

5. Add the olive oil to the pan the Venison was in and add the ginger and half the spring onions and fry for 2-3 mins on the simmering plate.

6. Add the blanched green veg and fry for 2 mins. Have another sip.

7. Pour in the sauce and bring it to a gentle bubble and mix the ingredients really well.

8. Now add the Venison to the same pan, stir well, scatter over the remaining spring onions and fresh dill then serve immediately with rice or noodles or even a fresh crisp salad, a squeeze of lime and a great big kiss.

9. Have a good slug of Rosé and enjoy with your beloved!

Venison Rice Bowl

This is a scrumptious bowl of comfort food - perfect for cosy nights in with a movie.

For 4 people, you will need:

- 600g Venison Minute Steaks
- 1 tbsp olive oil
- 2 garlic cloves, crushed
- 2 onions, halved and finely sliced
- 2 spring onions, finely sliced
- 1 packet cherry tomatoes, some halved and some quartered
- 4 tbsp sweet chilli sauce
- 2 mugs brown rice

Method:

1. Cut the venison Minute Steaks into finger sized slices.
2. Pop on the rice to cook following the packet instructions.
3. Heat a non stick frying pan on the simmering plate and add the olive oil. When it is hot add the onions and fry gently until they are soft and golden.
4. Add in the garlic and half the sliced spring onions mix well then add in the cherry tomatoes and stir.
5. Cook gently for 10 mins then move the pan to the hot plate to crank up the heat and add in the sliced venison, mixing well. Once it has browned add the sweet chilli sauce, transfer the pan to the simmering plate and mix well.
6. Tip the cooked and drained rice into the pan, combine it all together gently and serve in four bowls, topped with the remaining spring onions.
7. Enjoy with a movie and a comfy sofa.

Ultimate Venison Sandwich

These are fab Saturday lunch sandwiches – do add the condiment of your choice, we love grainy mustard or horseradish.

For 4 people, you will need:

- 600g Venison Minute Steaks
- 3 tbsp olive oil
- 2 red onions halved then finely sliced
- 2 parsnips peeled and cut into little finger sized chunks
- 2 garlic cloves, finely sliced
- 4 small baguettes or 1 long baguette cut into quarters

Method:

1. Pop 2 tablespoons of olive oil into an oven proof dish and add in the onions, garlic and parsnips

2. Roast for 20 mins until the parsnips are soft

3. Meanwhile, pop the baguettes in the baking oven for a few minutes to warm

4. Take a non stick frying pan, add a tablespoon of olive oil and when it is hot flash fry the steaks for 30 seconds. Remove them from the heat, place on a board and leave them to rest for a couple of minutes before slicing them lengthways.

5. Remove the baguettes from the oven, butter them and add on the onions, parsnips and top with the steaks.

Teriyaki Venison with Noodles

There are quite a few ingredients in this recipe and you do need to plan ahead but I promise, it is simple. The flavours sing and the noodles ensure it is a crowd pleaser!

For 4 people, you will need:

- 600g Venison Minute Steaks
- Vegetables cut into strips for stir frying (red onions, peppers, baby corn, green beans, broccoli florets, whatever you have in the fridge)
- 300g fresh beansprouts (you could use a drained can of beansprouts from the store cupboard if you prefer)
- 600g noodles, cooked according to the instructions on the packet

For the Teriyaki Sauce you will need:

- 200ml cold water
- 1 heaped tsp cornflour
- 5 tbsp soy sauce
- 5 tbsp runny honey
- 1 tbsp fish sauce
- 1 tsp ground ginger
- 1 tsp roasted garlic granules
- 1 tsp Lazy Chilli
- 2 tbsp olive oi

Method:

1. Start by popping the cold water in a bowl, add in the cornflour then mix well until dissolved and the water is cloudy. Now add the rest of the Teriyaki sauce ingredients. Place the Minute Steaks in a flat deep baking tray/casserole dish and then pour the sauce over the steaks. Leave to marinade for at least 4 hours.

2. When you are ready to cook, slice up your chosen vegetables, add a tablespoon of olive oil to a non stick pan and stir-fry them on the hot plate until just cooked so they still have a crunch. Add in the beansprouts then tip into a bowl and set aside but keep warm in the simmering oven.

3. Cook the noodles according to the packet and set aside.

4. Again using the non-stick pan, pop in a further tablespoon of olive oil. When the pan is hot, add the Minute Steaks, and after 30 seconds turn them over then add in all the marinade and mix well.

5. Remove the steaks to a chopping board and slice them into finger size pieces. Leave the sauce in the pan and keep warm.

6. Mix the noodles and the vegetables together.

7. Take a large platter and place the noodles and veg on it, spreading them out. Top with the sliced venison and drizzle with the sauce.

8. Serve in the middle of a table with friends and plenty of chatter.

Venison Apricot Couscous

This is a fabulous light Summer dish which can be enjoyed as part of a buffet or as a lunch with salad.

It is a useful recipe for your Venison toolbox as you can use either minute steaks, steaks, fillet for a special occasion or simply use leftovers from a roast. It uses simple store cupboard ingredients but if you did want to use fresh tomatoes then please do.

For 4 people, you will need:

- 600g Venison Minute Steaks
- 2 tbsp olive oil
- 1 red onion, diced
- 300g couscous
- 1 tbsp harissa paste
- 1 chicken stock cube
- 8 dried apricots, halved
- 8 sun dried tomatoes, halved
- 2 limes, juice and zest
- Fresh coriander
- Fresh basil

Method:

1. Cook the couscous according to the instructions on the packet using boiling water and pop in the chicken stock cube.

2. Heat the olive oil in a non stick pan and add the diced onions and gently fry until soft on the simering plate.

3. Cut the minute steaks into small finger slices and flash fry them in the pan on the hot plate with the onions.

4. Add the harissa paste, apricots and sun dried tomatoes to the pan. Mix well and squeeze in the juice of 1 lime.

5. Now add the cooked couscous to the pan of Venison, fluff it up and mix it through.

6. Squeeze over the juice of the second lime then sprinkle over the zest and herbs, mix well and serve.

Zingy Lime Curry

For 4 people, you will need:

- 600g Venison Minute Steaks
- 1 tbsp olive oil
- 1 tsp Lazy Chilli
- 1 tsp Lazy Ginger
- 2 red onions halved and finely sliced
- 5 garlic cloves, crushed
- 6 limes
- 100ml chicken stock
- 1 can full fat coconut milk
- 1 mug peas
- Fresh dill

Method:

1. Put the olive oil in a non stick deep frying pan and place on the hot plate. When hot add the lazy chilli, lazy ginger, garlic and the onions. Move the pan to the simmering plate, fry gently for 8-10 minutes until the onions are golden brown.

2. Add in the zest and juice of 5 limes and mix well.

3. Cut the Minute Steaks into finger width sizes, put the pan back on the hot plate and brown the meat quickly stirring well. When the meat is brown, return the pan to the simmering plate.

4. Now add in the peas, stock and the can of coconut milk and bring to the boil gently then simmer until the liquid has reduced by about half. This should take around 20 minutes.

5. Serve with sticky rice and a wedge of lime. Scatter the fresh dill over the top and serve immediately.

Minute Steaks with a Beetroot and Orange Salad

Venison is so simple and versatile and this is another recipe which could use Minute Steaks, Steaks or fillet – whichever you prefer.

For 4 people, you will need:

- 600g Venison Minute Steaks
- 300g beetroot cut into small finger sizes
- 4 oranges
- 50g fresh watercress
- 1 tbsp cider vinegar
- 1 bag rocket
- 4 tbsp olive oil
- 1 tbsp freshly chopped coriander
- 1 tsp Bo Tree Black Pepper
- 1 tsp Himalayan Salt

Method:

1. Peel the beetroot, cut it into small finger pieces, pop it in a roasting tin, drizzle with a tablespoon of olive oil and roast for 25 minutes in the roasting oven.

2. Whisk together the cider vinegar with salt and pepper and 3 tablespoons of olive oil

3. Once roasted, spread the beetroot over a platter and sprinkle with a tablespoon of the dressing.

4. Peel the oranges, finely slice them and then cut into small chunks

5. Flash fry the minute steaks for 30 seconds on each side then leave to rest. Then chop into finger sized slices.

6. Arrange the rocket, beetroot chunks, oranges chunks and watercress on a platter, slice the venison steaks and place on top then scatter over the rest of the dressing and the coriander.

Venison, Leeks & Parmesan Spaghetti

This is a simple, fast supper recipe – I like to use fancy pasta I have bought on holiday but any shape and colour will do!

For 4 people, you will need:

- 600g Venison Minute Steaks sliced into finger sized slices
- 2 tbsp olive oil
- 2 fresh leeks cut into chunky slices
- 200ml double cream
- 1 tbsp fresh parsley or coriander or dill
- 2 garlic cloves crushed
- 500g pasta of your choice
- 150g Parmesan cheese finely grated

Method:

1. Pop the pasta on to cook following the instructions on the packet.
2. Heat up a large non stick pan on the hot plate and when hot sear the Venison for 30 seconds on each side then remove from the pan and set aside.
3. Now add the olive oil and when hot, add the leeks and garlic, stir then move the pan to the simmering plate and cook gently until soft.
4. Once soft, add the cream, herbs and stir well.
5. Add the Venison, stir well and reduce the heat.
6. Drain the cooked pasta and mix it into the Venison and add a table spoon of the pasta water and mix really well. Pop the pan back on the hot plate, stir for 2 minutes then season, scatter over the parmesan cheese and serve with garlic bread, yum!

Katsu Minute Steaks

This is a great recipe for zingy Minute Steaks but is equally delicious using left overs from a Venison roast too. It does look like there are a lot of ingredients but I promise, it is simple!

For 4 people, you will need:

For the sauce:

- 3 tbsp Katsu paste
- 2 tbsp clear runny honey
- 1 tbsp olive oil

For the meat bowl:

- 600g Venison minute steaks cut into strips
- 2 tbsp olive oil
- 4 eggs
- 4 spring onions, finely sliced
- 2 tsp ground ginger
- 1 tbsp dark soy sauce
- 2 carrots, grated
- 300g bag of beansprouts
- 1 red onion finely sliced
- 600g fresh noodles
- 1 tbsp fresh dill finely chopped

Method:

1. Whisk together all the sauce ingredients and set aside.
2. Cook the noodles according to the packet instructions and put to the side.
3. Next, it's time to fry the eggs so pop a tablespoon of olive oil in a frying pan and heat it up on the simmering plate. Crack the eggs into the pan, and fry until the whites have set but yolks are still wobbly.
4. Heat another frying pan, pop in a further tablespoon of olive oil and add the venison strips with the ginger, soy sauce and brown fast. Add in the vegetables and beansprouts and cook stirring constantly for 5 minutes.
5. Now add the noodles and mix well.
6. Spoon over the sauce and stir fry for 2 minutes until everything is coated and glossy.
7. To serve, divide it all between 4 bowls and top each with an egg. Sprinkle over some fresh dill and enjoy!

Garlicky Paprika Pasta Bake

Children and adults alike love this recipe – go on, give it a go!

For 4 people, you will need:

- 600g Venison minute steaks cut into finger size pieces
- 1 tbsp olive oil
- 1 onion, finely sliced
- 1 courgette cut into 1cm chunks
- 4 garlic cloves, crushed
- 1 onion finely sliced
- 3 tsp paprika
- 1 litre passata sauce
- 1 tin sweetcorn, drained and rinsed
- 200ml chicken stock
- 400g pasta (not spaghetti)
- 100g cheddar cheese
- 50g parmesan cheese

Method:

1. In a heavy based pan, add the olive oil, pop in on the simmering plate and when hot add the onions and garlic and sauté gently. Add in the Venison, transfer to the hot plate and brown fast all over.

2. Pop in the courgette and the sweetcorn and stir well for 5 minutes.

3. Add in the paprika, stir well and cook for 2 minutes.

4. Pour in the passata sauce, hot stock and bring to a simmer. Allow to bubble for 10 minutes then pop on the lid and bang it in the baking oven for 20 minutes. Remove, stir in 50g of the cheddar cheese, put the lid back on and place back in the simmering oven for 10 minutes.

5. Cook the pasta according to the instructions on the packet.

6. Take a large baking dish and pop in the pasta, pour over the venison mixture and stir well to ensure the pasta is well covered with the sauce. Cover with the remaining cheddar cheese and then top with the parmesan cheese.

7. Put this in the baking oven, uncovered, for 20 minutes or until the cheese is brown and bubbling.

8. Enjoy with lashings of garlic bread.

Page 111

Page 116

Page 119

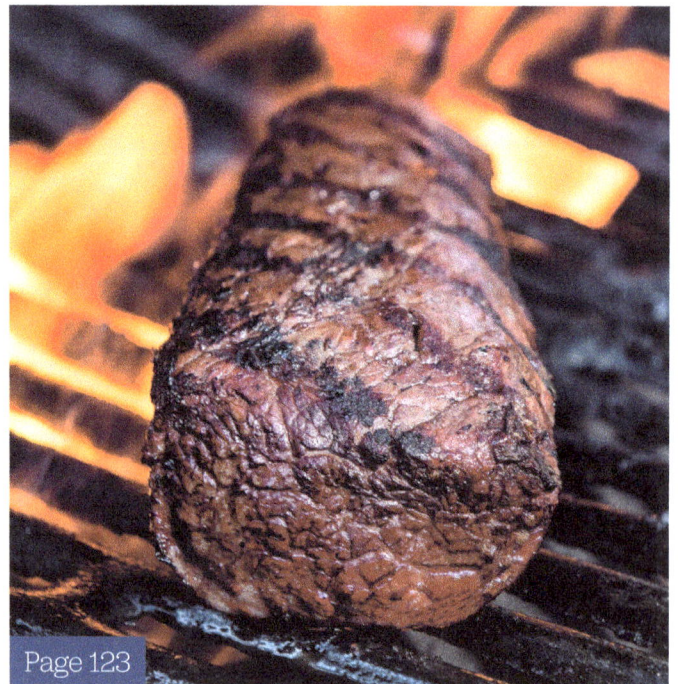
Page 123

BBQ

Venison is perfect for cooking on the barbecue as salads compliment it beautifully.

Venison burgers and sausages are of course barbecue staples and we always make sure that we have these available when barbecuing but I do like to make it more interesting by adding fillets, kebabs or steaks.

I make up BBQ Boxes and pop them in the freezer so when the sun decides to shine in Scotland, I am all ready to go and don't have to do a mad dash to the supermarket and spend all day in the kitchen.

Generally these recipes are for 4 people but of course, if you want to double it up for more people simply multiply out the ingredients appropriately. It goes without saying that you must defreeze the boxes overnight and ensure the meat is thoroughly defrosted before you start cooking. With Venison, remember the meat should be at room temperature before you start cooking to ensure it is succulent and tasty.

Do use the fillet recipes for the barbecue too and try the recipes in this chapter for a change – just add sunshine, blue sky and friends!

Marinated BBQ Venison Haunch Steaks

Serves 4

- 4 Venison Haunch Steaks
- 1 tbsp olive oil
- 130g Greek yoghurt
- 130g single cream
- 1 tsp paprika
- 1 tsp black pepper
- 1 tsp oregano
- 1 tbsp tomato puree
- 3 garlic cloves, peeled and crushed
- 2 tbsp lemon juice
- 2 tbsp olive oil
- Fresh chives to garnish

Method:

1. Make the marinade first so into a baking dish put the yoghurt, cream, paprika, pepper, oregano, tomato puree, garlic, lemon juice and one tablespoon of olive oil. Mix well with a whisk.

2. Pop in the steaks, ensure they are covered on all sides with the marinade, cover with cling film and leave in the fridge for as long as possible to marinade OR if they are going in the freezer pop everything into a container which has a tight-fitting lid and freeze it.

3. When ready, ensure the meat is at room temperature and cook the steaks on a hot barbecue for one and a half minutes on each side to ensure they are still pink in the middle.

4. Leave to rest for 5 minutes then serve with scrummy salad and sun!

Turkish Kebabs

Serves 4

For the kebabs

- 4 Venison haunch steaks cut up into 1 inch size cubes
- 2 red peppers, cut into chunks
- 2 yellow peppers, cut into chunks
- 2 red onions cut into chunks

For the marinade

- 4 tbsp olive oil
- 250ml natural yogurt
- 3 garlic cloves, peeled and crushed
- 2 tbsp lemon juice
- 1 tsp ground cumin
- 1 tsp dried oregano
- 1 tsp ground cinnamon
- $\frac{1}{2}$ tsp medium chilli powder
- 1 tsp salt
- 1 tsp ground black pepper

Method:

1. Mix all the marinade ingredients together in a large bowl.

2. Place the meat into the marinade and ensure it is well covered.

3. Leave to marinade in the fridge for at least 3 hours but preferably overnight. If you intend to freeze these then pop them in a container with a tight fitting lid before putting in the freezer.

4. When you are ready to start barbecuing, thread the Venison onto metal skewers, alternating with yellow and red pepper squares and adding on some onion too.

5. Ensure the meat is at room temperature and cook on a hot barbecue for 3 minutes on each side.

6. Serve with green salad, new potatoes and Baba Ghanoush.

BBQ Venison and Lentil Salad

This is a versatile recipe as although I use minute steaks here, fillet or even haunch steaks would also work beautifully.

Serves 4

- 600g Venison Minute Steaks
- 1 tbsp olive oil
- 1 tbsp Bo Tree White Pepper pearls
- 400g green/black lentils cooked according to the packet instructions
- Bag of salad from the supermarket or fresh salad from the garden
- Jar of sun dried tomatoes
- Half a red onion finely sliced
- 1 tbsp fresh mint leaves
- A lemon

Dressing:

- 100g Greek Style Yoghurt
- 1 tbsp fresh mint
- 1 garlic clove, peeled and crushed
- Half a cucumber, diced with the middle part spooned out

Method:

1. Put the olive oil and Bo Tree White pepper in a bowl. Put the Venison into a baking dish and cover with the mixture and marinade for at least 3 hours.
2. Cook the lentils as per the packet instructions.
3. Once cooked, drain the lentils and add in the finely sliced fresh red onions, half the mint leaves and sun dried tomatoes from the jar which should be sliced in half, length ways.
4. Make the dressing by mixing together all the ingredients and set this aside.
5. When ready to eat, ensure the meat is at room temperature and cook the Minute Steaks on the barbecue for 20 seconds each side. Leave to rest for 2-3 minutes then slice the venison at an angle.
6. To plate up, take a large platter and pop on the salad leaves, then spoon over the lentil salad, top with the Venison then drizzle over the dressing and squeeze the juice of the lemon over the top. Finally sprinkle over the last fresh mint leaves.
7. Serve in the middle of the table with lashings of Rosé wine!

Sticky Mango BBQ Skewers

These are a fab way to spice up your BBQ.

Serves 4

- 4 Venison haunch steaks cut into 1 inch size chunks
- 1 tbsp olive oil
- 3 tbsp mango chutney
- 3 tbsp mild curry powder
- 3 garlic cloves, crushed
- 1 red pepper cut into chunks
- 1 yellow pepper cut into chunks
- 1 red onion cut into chunks

Method:

1. Pop the Venison into a bowl and add in the olive oil, the mango chutney, curry powder and garlic. Mix well so the meat is evenly coated. Marinade overnight if possible but at least for 3 hours. If they are going in the freezer pop everything into a container which has a tight-fitting lid and freeze it.

2. When ready to start barbecuing take your skewers and thread on a pepper chunk then a piece of Venison then a different colour of pepper and some onion in turn down the length of the skewer.

3. Once the barbecue is hot, pop on the skewers and cook on each side for 3 minutes.

4. Serve with a couscous salad.

Surf & Turf

This is a show stopping barbecue bobby-dazzler!

Serves 4

- 4 Venison haunch steaks
- 1 tbsp olive oil
- 1 tbsp peppercorns
- 20 large tiger prawns
- 2 lemons

Method:

1. Take a large plate and put a tablespoon of olive oil on it and pour over 1 tablespoon of ground black peppercorns and mix.

2. Now pop the steaks on the plate and ensure they are well covered in the olive oil and pepper on both sides. Remember the steaks must be at room temperature before you start cooking them.

3. Thread the prawns onto skewers.

4. Juice one of the lemons, cover the prawns with the juice then pop them on the hot barbecue and cook them until pink and delicious. Set them to one side.

5. Pop the steaks on the barbecue for one and a half minutes each side then leave to rest for 3 minutes.

6. Get your plates, pop the steak in the middle, top with 5 prawns each and then cut the second lemon to give everyone a slice on their plate so they can squeeze more lovely juices over the top.

7. Enjoy with friends, in the garden with a fresh rocket salad and plenty of chatter.

Chilli Kebabs

These kebabs are an absolute weekend winner – quick to prepare and easy to cook on a the BBQ or if the weather isn't obliging, they work beautifully on the griddle pan too.

Serves 4

- 4 Venison haunch steaks cut into 1 inch size chunks
- 1 can of chopped pineapple (or chunks of fresh pineapple if you have it)
- 1 tbsp fresh basil
- 2 tbsp garlic puree
- 3 tbsp mild chilli powder
- 1 tsp Lazy Chilli
- 2 tbsp olive oil

Method:

1. In a large bowl, mix all the ingredients together and leave to marinade for as long as possible – over night is best but for at least 3 hours will work.
2. When ready to cook, as always ensure the meat is at room temperature and pop the meat on to the skewers adding a pineapple chunk between each piece of meat.
3. Barbecue the skewers for 3 minutes on each side.
4. Serve with delicious salad and wild rice.

BBQ Fillet

Venison Fillet is brilliant on the barbecue – super simple and very impressive when it is sliced and arranged on a platter with salad for everyone to dig in. We like to add spices from the Bo Tree Pepper range. The Herb de Kampot is our favourite as it is gentle so allows the mellow Venison flavour to come through. You will of course have your own favourite spices which you may wish to use. Often good quality freshly ground pepper is perfect.

Serves 4

- 500g Venison fillet
- 2 tbsp olive oil
- 2 tbsp Herbs de Kampot

Method:

1. Take a large plate and add the olive oil, spices and mix well.
2. Put the filet on that plate and coat it in the oil mixture.
3. When ready to cook ensure the meat is at room temperature.
4. Once the barbecue is hot, sear the fillet on each side for 3 minutes then leave to rest on a board for around 5-8 minutes before slicing. We like our Venison on the rare side.

Page 127

Page 131

Page 132

Page 135

Page 136

Page 139

Page 140

Page 144

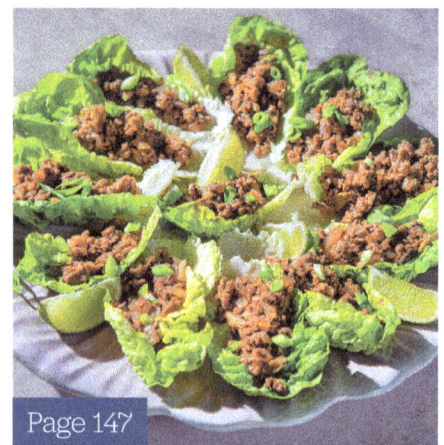
Page 147

Mince

Venison Mince is a staple in my kitchen as it is so versatile: add carrots and onions to make a traditional Stalker's Pie (the Venison version of Shepherd's or Cottage pie), passata and herbs to be more Italian or for a taste of the Orient add exciting sauces like fish, soy or hoisin.

These are a collection of our firm family favourites – I hope your family enjoys them too!

Moroccan Chilli

I have suggested a large batch for this so that you can either feed a houseful or pop half in the freezer for another time – like all spicy recipes, this always tastes better the following day!

For 10 - 12 people you will need:

- 1.5kg Venison mince
- 3 tbsp olive oil
- 2 tsp ground cumin
- 3 onions halved and thinly sliced
- 2 tbsp ground ginger
- 6 garlic cloves, peeled and crushed
- 2 tins chopped tomatoes
- 1 litre passata sauce
- 2 tbsp paprika
- 1 tbsp ground cinnamon
- 2 tsp ground coriander
- 3 tbsp harissa paste
- 2 cans kidney beans, drained and rinsed
- 3 peppers – red yellow and orange, diced
- 400ml beef stock
- Fresh coriander to garnish

Method:

1. Take a large heavy based pan, pour in 2 tablespoons of the olive oil and heat on the simmering plate. Add in the ground cumin and fry gently for 2 minutes. Add the further tablespoon of olive oil, pop in the chopped onions and fry gently for 5 minutes.

2. Move the pan to the hot plate, add in the ginger, garlic and Venison mince, breaking it up.

3. After around 20 minutes the mince should be brown, so now add in the tomatoes, passata, remaining spices and the harissa.

4. Mix well and add in the kidney beans, peppers and beef stock.

5. Cover with a tight-fitting lid and bring to the boil then pop in the simmering oven for 2 hours.

6. Serve with rice, fresh coriander and sour cream.

MiMi's Meatballs of Fire

Meatballs are always such a hit with the family – the children love to get involved in helping make them and of course they freeze well. I frequently rely on this recipe as it uses lots of trusty store cupboard ingredients which is always helpful, especially for a last minute supper. This makes around 16 little meatballs.

For 4 people you will need:

- 500g Venison mince
- 1 tbsp olive oil
- 1 tbsp medium spice paste
- 1 tsp Lazy Chilli
- 2 tsp garlic puree
- Beansprouts (fresh if you have them)
- 1 jar of Lime Pickle
- 500g Natural Yoghurt
- 1 lime cut into wedges

Method:

1. Place the Venison mince into a large bowl and break it up – children love to use their fingers!

2. Add in the spice paste, chilli and garlic and mix well with the back of a fork.

3. Use a teaspoon as a measure to make up the meatballs – I like making little meatballs as they cook quicker. Scoop a teaspoon of mince into your hand and rub it into a little ball.

4. Heat the oil in a heavy based pan on the hot plate and once hot add in the meatballs and cook on all sides for around 4-5 minutes.

5. Once they are cooked and a lovely deep brown colour, remove and place on a warmed plate in the simmering oven.

6. To the heavy based pan, add the lime pickle, mix well soaking up the lovely bits from the bottom of the pan and then add the yogurt and mix well warming gently.

7. Take your serving platter and put the beansprouts on the bottom, then add the meatballs and top with the sauce. Place the lime wedges around the side and serve.

Pitscandly Stalkers Pie

This is of course a Venison farmer's version of Shepherd's or Cottage Pie as we are using Venison mince instead of lamb or beef mince. This recipe is full of traditional, strong flavours accompanied by comforting mash.

For an 8 person pie you will need:

- 1 kg Venison mince
- 2 tbsp olive oil
- 2 red onions finely diced
- 3 garlic cloves, peeled and crushed
- 4 carrots, peeled and cubed
- 2 beef Oxo cubes
- 500ml beef stock
- 4 tbsp Worcestershire sauce
- 1 tbsp tomato puree
- 1 tbsp dried parsley
- 200g cheddar cheese

For the mash:

- 1.5kg potatoes
- 200ml milk
- 25g butter

Method:

1. Heat a heavy based pan on the simmering plate and add in the olive oil, onions and garlic. Allow them to sauté gently then once soft, move the pan to the hot plate, add in the mince and brown it well – depending on the size of your pan you may need to do this in batches.

2. Once browned, crumble over the Oxo cubes and stir well.

3. Now add in the Worcestershire sauce, dried parsley and tomato puree and again stir well.

4. Pop in the carrots and pour over the stock. Bring it all to the boil, put on the lid and place it in the simmering oven for 2 hours.

5. Meantime, peel and chop the potatoes then, cover them in water and boil them up with a pinch of salt until cooked. Drain them then add in the butter and mash well. Add the milk in 50ml at a time mashing well.

6. Once the mince is cooked, take a baking dish and pop the mixture in the bottom of the dish, top with the mash, using the back of a fork to get good ridges in a tartan effect then top with the cheese.

7. Pop in the baking oven for 40 minutes until the top is brown and bubbling. If you think it is browning too fast cover with foil.

8. Serve with peas if you fancy some extra veg.

Greek Meatballs with Tzatziki

Summery and scrumptious - these meatballs are divine.

You will need for 4 people:

- 500g Venison mince (this will make around 16 little meatballs)
- 1 tbsp olive oil
- red onion finely diced
- 2 garlic cloves, peeled and crushed
- 1 lime – the zest only for the mince
- 2 tbsp dried oregano
- 1 tbsp full fat Greek yoghurt
- 2 tbsp tomato puree

You will need for the Tzatziki

- Half a cucumber, grated (remember to discard the watery centre)
- 2 garlic cloves, peeled and crushed
- 300g Greek yoghurt
- 2 tbsp lime juice
- 1 tbsp chopped mint leaves

Method:

1. In a large bowl add in the Venison mince, crushed garlic, diced onion, lime zest, oregano, tomato puree and the Greek yoghurt then mix well – with your hands is best or use the back of a fork. It will be smelling scrumptious.

2. Make little meat balls by using a teaspoon to measure the mince mixture into your hand before rolling into a ball. You should get 16 little balls of gorgeousness.

3. Pop all the little meatballs on a cold tray, and place in the fridge for an hour to firm up.

4. While they are chilling, make the Tzatziki by grating the cucumber into a bowl (try and just grate the hard bit and discard the soft centre as it is too watery for the sauce). Add the garlic, yoghurt and lime juice. Mix well and season then add the fresh mint leaves.

5. When you are ready to cook, heat a non-stick pan on the hot plate and add in the olive oil. Once it is hot, add the meatballs but cook them in batches so there is enough space in the pan to turn them around so they cook and go brown on all sides. This should take around 4-5 minutes on all sides.

6. Once cooked, remove and place on kitchen paper to remove excess fat.

7. To serve, pop on a serving platter with salad, scatter over any extra mint leaves and put the Tzatziki in the middle ready for dipping. I love to warm pitta breads and slice them into finger slices to serve beside the tzatziki ready for dipping too.

8. Enjoy with a glass of something white and crisp.

Farm Bolognaise

Spag Bol is always a winner with the family and Venison mince makes a really scrumptious bolognaise sauce.

For 4 people you will need:

- 500g Venison mince
- 1 tbsp olive oil
- 3 garlic cloves, peeled and crushed
- 2 tbsp tomato puree
- 1 onion, finely diced
- 1 stalk of celery, finely diced
- 2 carrots, finely diced
- 1 beef Oxo cube, crumbled
- 2 tbsp mushroom ketchup
- 400ml passata sauce
- 1 large glass of red wine
- 1 tbsp dried Italian herbs
- Parmesan cheese to serve

Method:

1. Put the olive oil in a heavy based pan (which has a tight-fitting lid) and heat it gently on the simmering plate. When hot, add the onions and garlic and soften.

2. Move the pan to the hot plate and pop in the mince and brown rapidly, breaking it up with a wooden spoon.

3. When it is brown, add the mushroom ketchup, tomato puree and crumble over the Oxo cube then pour in the red wine and mix well.

4. Add in the diced celery and carrot then pour over the passata sauce.

5. Mix well and allow it to bubble. Scatter over the herbs then pop on the lid.

6. Place the pan in the baking oven for an hour then enjoy with lots of pasta, parmesan cheese, garlic bread and salad.

Spicy Mini Naan Breads

This is a fun food platter which is perfect for a Summer alfresco lunch or supper. I would prefer to scatter pomegranate seeds over the top however these are not always available in Forfar so I tend to use red peppers. However, if you can find those luscious seeds – please do use them!

For 4 people you will need:

- 500g Venison mince
- 1 tbsp olive oil
- 1 red onion, finely diced
- 2 garlic cloves, peeled and crushed
- $\frac{1}{2}$ tsp ground cinnamon
- 1 tsp zaatar
- 3 tsp dried coriander leaf
- 1 red pepper, finely diced (or pomegranate seeds)
- 1 tbsp fresh coriander
- 1 tbsp fresh mint
- 1 tsp dried parsley
- $\frac{1}{2}$ tsp ground coriander
- 1 Beef oxo cube, crumbled
- 8 cherry tomatoes, quartered
- Packet of 6 garlic and coriander mini naan breads

Serve with a dressing :

- 1 tbsp grated cucumber
- 1 tbsp natural yoghurt
- 1 lemon – juice and rind

Method:

1. Mix the dressing ingredients together in a bowl and set aside.
2. Heat the olive oil in a non-stick pan on the hot plate then add the diced onion and garlic then move to the simmering plate.
3. Gently fry until soft and golden.
4. Move the pan back to the hotplate. Add the Venison mince and break it up mixing it well. Cook for 10 minutes until brown and cooked.
5. Add in the cinnamon and zaatar, mix well and allow to cook for 5 minutes.
6. Now add in the crumbled Oxo cube, dried coriander leaf, dried parsley and cook for another 5 minutes then pop in the simmering oven for 15 minutes.
7. Cut the mini naan breads in half width ways and warm according to the packet instructions.
8. Once warm, place them on a large platter, pop the mince over each naan bread and scatter the finely diced red pepper (or pomegranate seeds) over the mince.
9. Drizzle the dressing over the top.
10. Sprinkle over the fresh herbs and place the little tomato quarters around the platter.

Swedish Meatballs

For 4 people you will need:

- 500g Venison mince
- 1 tbsp olive oil
- 1 onion diced
- 1 tsp butter
- 1 tsp flour
- 1 tsp all spice
- 200ml chicken stock
- 175ml double cream
- Squeeze of lemon
- 2 tbsp of Worcestershire sauce
- Fresh dill

Method:

1. In a large bowl mix the mince, 1 tbsp Worcestershire sauce and diced onion together then form into balls using a soupspoon to get the amount correct. I prefer these meatballs larger than the other recipes but if you would prefer smaller ones do use a teaspoon.

2. Heat the olive oil on the hot plate in a non-stick pan and brown the meatballs well all over which will take around 20 minutes, then remove and pop them on a preheated plate and place in the simmering oven.

3. Transfer the pan to the simmering plate, add the butter and melt. Whisk in the plain flour to make a paste then add the all spice and cook until smelling gorgeous

4. Gradually add in the chicken stock whisking well then finally add in the cream remembering to keep whisking. You should now have a lovely thick glossy sauce.

5. Return the meatballs to the pan, mix them into the sauce, cover with a tight-fitting lid and simmer gently for 15 minutes.

6. Remove from the heat, squeeze in the lemon juice and sprinkle over the final tablespoon of Worcestershire sauce and serve with lashings of mashed potato and sprinkle with chopped fresh dill.

Venison Lime Noodles

This is a really quick and delicious way to cook Venison Mince which everyone will adore. I like to serve it on a large platter in the middle of the table so everyone can dig in and help themselves. The secret to this recipe is to have lots of limes to use both during the cooking and for serving.

For 4 people you will need:

- 500g Venison mince
- 1 tbsp olive oil
- 3 garlic cloves, peeled and crushed
- 1 onion, finely diced
- 3 tbsp soy sauce
- 200g jar of red Thai paste
- 4 spring onions, finely sliced
- 4 limes
- 3 handfuls of frozen peas
- 1 can of coconut milk
- 150ml chicken stock
- 600g Rice Noodles

Method:

1. Heat the olive oil in a non-stick pan on the hot plate and add the Venison mince , the juice of 2 of the limes and mix well ensuring the juices soak in and the mince browns well.

2. Add in the garlic and onions and continue to break up the Venison mince and mix well. Move to the simmering plate and cook gently for 8-10 minutes, stirring occasionally.

3. Now add in the soy sauce, red Thai paste and half the spring onions.

4. Mix well and then add in the hot stock. Bubble for 5 minutes then add in the coconut milk.

5. Cover with a lid, move to the simmering plate and simmer for 10 minutes.

6. Add in the frozen peas and cook for a further 10 minutes.

7. Meanwhile, cook the rice noodles in accordance with the packet instructions then drain.

8. Pop the noodles onto a platter, top with the Venison and drizzle the juice of a further lime over the top. Cut the final lime into wedges and arrange around the sides of the platter. Sprinkle the remaining spring onions over the top with a final flourish and enjoy with friends and fizz!

Moussaka

Venison mince makes a delicious Moussaka so I strongly recommend you have a go at this simple version of a classic recipe. I am a busy working mum so don't always have time to make my own bechamel sauce - you can decide what suits you best, no judgements here!

For 4 people you will need:

- 500g Venison mince
- 2 tbsp olive oil
- 3 aubergines sliced into circles around 1cm thick
- 2 red onions, diced
- 3 cloves of garlic, peeled and crushed
- 1 beef Oxo cube
- $\frac{1}{2}$ tsp Lazy Chilli
- 2 tsp cinnamon
- 2 tsp dried oregano
- 1 bay leaf
- 200ml red wine
- 500ml passata sauce
- 2 tbsp tomato puree
- 500g potatoes peeled and also sliced into 1cm circles

Bechamel Sauce
(cheat and buy this if you are tight for time!)

- 950ml full fat milk
- 110g salted butter
- 6 tablespoons plain flour

Method:

1. Place a non-stick frying pan on the hot plate. When hot, fry the slices of aubergine until they are golden brown and soft. Remove and set aside for later.

2. In a heavy based pan which has a tight-fitting lid, add the olive oil and heat fast on the hot plate. Add the onions and garlic and soften. Then add the Venison mince browning it well and breaking it up so there are no chunks.

3. Now add in the herbs, Lazy Chili, bay leaf and mix well, continuing to break up the mince.

4. Crumble in the Oxo cube and pour in the wine. Mix well.

5. Add the tomato puree and passata sauce then bring to the boil.

6. Replace the lid and pop in the baking oven for an hour and then move the pan to the simmering oven for a further hour.

7. Meanwhile, part boil the potatoes then remove from the water, cut into circles and put them aside.

8. Now make the Bechamel sauce (or open the jar!): melt the butter in a small non-stick saucepan, stir in the flour and cook over a medium heat for a couple of minutes and then remove from the heat and slowly pour in the milk whilst whisking vigorously. Once the sauce is smooth return it to the heat and bring to a simmer for a few minutes then season well. You're finished, phew!

9. Back to the Moussaka and it's time to assemble it. Get a large rectangular ovenproof dish and add a third of the meat (remember to remove the bay leaf) to it and spread out evenly, top with half the aubergine and half the potato, then layer with the rest of the meat and top with the remaining aubergine and potatoes. Cover with the bechamel sauce and pop in the roasting oven for 30 minutes and then transfer to the baking oven for another 30 mins ensuring it is golden brown and hot throughout before serving.

Thai Venison with Fried Egg

This is such a happy Saturday night recipe - do give it a go!

For 4 people you will need:

- 500g Venison mince
- 3 tbsp olive oil
- 4 garlic cloves, peeled and crushed
- 2 tsp of Lazy Chilli (more if you like it really hot!)
- 2 tbsp light soy sauce
- 2 tsp fish sauce
- 2 red onions, finely diced
- 1 beef Oxo cube
- 200g peas, cooked
- 1 handful of chopped coriander
- 4 free range eggs

Method:

1. Heat 2 tablespoons of olive oil in a heavy based frying pan on the simmering plate then add the garlic, Lazy Chilli, onions and fry until soft and golden. Have a sip of wine.

2. Move the pan to the hot plate, add the Venison mince and mix together, browning the mince, breaking up any lumps rapidly.

3. Crumble in the Oxo cube and again mix well.

4. Pour in the soy and fish sauce and then stir well for a couple of minutes, continuing to brown the mince and ensure it is cooked through.

5. Enjoy a sip of wine.

6. Stir through the cooked peas and season well. Add in the fresh herbs, mix well and transfer to a warmed bowl and place in the warming oven.

7. Add the final tablespoon of oil to the frying pan (which should still have all the yummy flavours from the mince), heat fast on the hot plate and fry the eggs.

8. To serve, place jasmine or sticky rice into 4 bowls, add the spicy Thai mince and top each bowl with a fried egg.

9. Have another sip of wine and enjoy!

Spicy Summer Mince Cups

I think this is a perfect way to use Venison mince to spice up Summer - it is a wonderful, colourful meal or alternatively, if you use smaller Baby Cos salad leaves, it is a fun Summer nibble for garden parties.

For 8 people you will need:

- 1kg Venison mince
- 2 tbsp olive oil
- 2 red onions, finely diced
- 6 garlic cloves, peeled and crushed
- 3 tsp ground ginger
- 4 tbsp oyster sauce
- 2 tbsp fish sauce
- 2 spring onions, finely diced
- 2 tsp Lazy Chilli
- 8 limes
- Cos or Baby Cos lettuce leaves
- Fresh coriander to garnish

Method:

1. Heat the olive oil in a heavy based pan on the hot plate then add the finely diced red onion and crushed garlic. Move the pan to the simmering plate and stir well.

2. Once the onions have softened, move the pan back to the hot plate and pop in the Venison mince, brown it fast breaking up any lumps, to ensure it has an even consistency. Have a lovely sip of Rosé.

3. Once it is browned, add in the oyster sauce, fish sauce, ginger and lazy chilli. Mix well and ensure it is still cooking fast.

4. Add three quarters of the spring onions and mix well together, still bashing the mince to ensure there are no lumps.

5. Pop the lid on and put in the simmering oven for 20 minutes while you break off the Cos lettuce leaves and arrange on a large plate. Cut up 5 of the limes into wedges and arrange between the lettuce.

6. Spoon the spicy Venison mince into each Cos leaf cup - you should just need a desert spoon in each but it depends on the size of the lettuce leaf. Scatter over the remaining spring onions and chopped fresh coriander then squeeze the juice of the final 3 limes all over the mince cups.

7. Have some more Rosé and place the platter in the middle of the table for everyone to enjoy!

Scrumptious Spicy Venison Platter

This is another crowd pleaser – perfect for a lunch with friends.

For 4 people you will need:

- 500g Venison mince
- 1 tbsp olive oil
- 1 onion, finely sliced
- 3 garlic cloves, peeled and crushed
- 1 tsp Lazy Chilli
- 1 tbsp garam masala
- 1 tsp ground ginger
- 1 tsp turmeric
- 1 can chopped tomatoes
- 250ml water
- 200g frozen peas
- 100g frozen spinach
- 100g full fat natural yoghurt
- 1 lime
- Fresh coriander

To serve:

- extra yoghurt and coriander, lime wedges, naan bread

Method:

1. In a large non-stick pan, heat the oil on the simmering plate then add the onion and garlic. Fry gently for 5 minutes then add the chilies, garam masala, ginger and turmeric. Fry for a further 3-5 minutes.

2. Add in the Venison mince and fry for 8-10 minutes, breaking up any chunks and then add in the chopped tomatoes and water. Pop a lid on and simmer for 20 minutes.

3. Add the frozen peas and spinach and cook for a further 10 minutes.

4. Stir in the natural yoghurt, fresh coriander and the juice of half the lime.

5. Stir well then pop in a serving bowl, top with a dollop of yoghurt and sprinkle with coriander and serve with lime wedges and warm naan bread.

6. Add in lashings of chatter.

Harissa Stuffed Courgettes

I love using this recipe when our walled garden is bursting with yellow and green courgettes – it is bliss to cut and eat them straight away.

For 4 people you will need:

- 500g Venison mince
- 1 tbsp olive oil
- 2 courgettes cut in half length ways
- 1 onion, finely diced
- 1 tbsp roasted garlic granules
- 1 tbsp cumin seeds
- 1 jar (170g) of Rose Harissa
- 500g passata sauce
- 100ml water

Method:

1. Cut the courgettes length ways and scoop out the flesh but do leave some courgette to ensure there is a shell around $1/2$ cm wide. Chop up the flesh and discard any large seeds.

2. Heat the olive oil in a heavy based pan on the hot plate, add the onion and cook until it is soft. Then add the mince and chopped courgette flesh and cook until the meat is a deep brown.

3. Move the pan to the simmering plate, add the garlic granules and cumin, mixing well and cook for 5 minutes.

4. Pop in the Harissa and mix well. Add 100ml of water to the Harissa jar and mix it well to ensure every last bit of Harissa is removed from the sides and pour that into the mince mixture too. Now add in the passata sauce and pop on a tight-fitting lid. Cook for a further 15 minutes on the simmering plate.

5. Take an ovenproof dish, pop in the courgettes and put them in the baking oven for 20 minutes to roast them.

6. Spoon the mince mixture into the roasted courgettes, cover with foil and bake in the baking oven for 30 minutes.

7. Serve with a lovely green salad.

Oriental Basil Mince

This is a super recipe for a light Summer lunch – it is zingy and bright, best served with a crisp rocket salad.

For 4 people you will need:

- 500g Venison mince
- 1 tbsp olive oil
- 1 red pepper, diced
- 2 shallots, finely diced
- 4 garlic cloves, peeled and crushed
- 2 limes
- 2 tbsp fish sauce
- 2 tsp soy sauce
- Bunch of fresh basil

Method:

1. Heat the olive oil in a non-stick pan and brown the mince on the hot plate bashing it well to ensure there are no chunks. Now remove it from the pan and place on a warmed plate or bowl and pop it in the simmering oven.

2. In the same pan now sauté the shallots and crushed garlic for 5 minutes on the simmering plate.

3. Add in the peppers and fry for a further 5 minutes.

4. Now add the browned mince back to the pan and toss in half the basil leaves, mix well, pop on a lid and leave for around 8 minutes on the simmering plate with the lid on.

5. Pour in the juice of one lime, fish sauce and soy sauce and mix well.

6. Replace the lid and fry for a further 10 minutes and then add in the rest of the fresh Basil, stir well then immediately serve with a lime wedge on the side.

Traditional Venison Chilli

I think it is important to include traditional flavours and recipes in this book as well as new ones and often, the oldies are the best! We enjoy this simple chilli throughout the year and I find it a real kitchen supper winner as I always have some in the freezer ready to go. The more condiments you have the fancier it becomes but it is still scrumptious with just some rice and a cheeky topping of cheese.

For 4 people you will need:

- 500g Venison mince
- 1 tbsp olive oil
- 1 red onion, finely diced
- 1 can of red kidney beans, drained and rinsed
- 1 litre passata sauce
- 1 tin of chopped tomatoes
- 3 garlic cloves, peeled and crushed
- 1 red pepper, diced
- 1 heaped tsp of Lazy Chilli (or more if you like it hot!)
- 1 beef Oxo cube crumbled

Method:

1. Heat the olive oil in a heavy based pan on the simmering plate.
2. When hot, add the diced red onion and garlic, gently frying until soft.
3. Add the mince and brown well breaking up any lumps – move the pan to the hot plate.
4. Once the mince is browned, add in the Lazy Chilli and mix well.
5. Crumble the Oxo cube over the mince and mix well.
6. Now add in the red pepper, kidney beans and stir it all together.
7. Add the passata sauce and tomatoes and once it bubbles, pop on the lid and place in the simmering oven for around 2 hours.
8. Enjoy with wild rice, sour cream, salad, grated cheese, friends and a rich glass of red.

Venison Sichuan with Noodles

This is a great way to use delicious Venison mince - bang a platter of this in the middle of the table and watch it disappear!

For 4 people you will need:

- 500g Venison mince
- 2 tbsp olive oil
- 3 garlic cloves, crushed
- 1 tsp Lazy Chilli
- 1 tbsp Chinese five spice
- 2 tsp sichuan peppercorns, crushed in a pestle and mortar
- 3 tbsp hoisin sauce
- 1 tbsp Muscovado sugar
- 5 tbsp soy sauce
- 100ml water
- 2 pak choi, halved
- 600g noodles
- 2 spring onions
- Fresh coriander

Method:

1. Put 1 tablespoon of olive oil in a non-stick, wide based pan and heat on the hot plate. Add the Venison mince and brown well breaking it up. This will take around 20 minutes.

2. Stir in the crushed garlic, Lazy Chilli, Chinese five spice, sichuan pepper and sugar. Mix well and cook until sizzling. Keep mixing it for around 5 minutes then remove the mixture and pop into a warmed bowl, cover with foil and place in the baking oven for 15 minutes.

3. In a separate bowl, mix the hoisin sauce, soy sauce and 100ml of water together.

4. Back to the non stick pan, and add to it, a further tablespoon of oil and once hot, add in the pak choi and fry in all the delicious Venison juices until tender.

5. Cook the noodles according to the instructions on the packet then drain and add to the non-stick pan with the pak choi. Add in the sauce from the separate bowl and mix well.

6. Put the sauce glazed noodles on a large platter, top with the Venison mince and scatter over the spring onions and fresh coriander.

7. Taa Daa! Enjoy with a crisp white wine.

Venison Lasagne

Everyone loves lasagne and Venison mince makes this extra specially scrumptious.

For 8 people you will need:

- 1kg of Venison mince
- 3 tbsp olive oil
- 1 red onion finely diced
- 100g chorizo sausage finely diced
- 2 red peppers diced
- 4 garlic cloves, peeled and crushed
- 2 litres passata sauce
- 2 beef Oxo cubes
- 400ml red wine
- 4 tsp mixed Italian dried herbs
- 2 jars of bechamel sauce (if you wish to make this from scratch do follow the instructions on page 143)
- 1 packet of fresh or dried lasagne pasta sheets
- 200g cheddar cheese
- 50g parmesan cheese

Method:

1. Take a heavy based pan and pop on the hot plate adding in the olive oil, onion and garlic. Cook for 3 minutes stirring constantly then add in the chorizo and transfer to the simmering plate and stir for a few minutes allowing the lovely red juices to escape.

2. Now add the mince to this pan– you may need to do this in batches to ensure it browns well breaking up any lumps to ensure consistency. This may take around 20 minutes.

3. Crumble in both Oxo cubes and stir well.

4. Now add in the peppers and red wine, mix well then allow to bubble for 5 minutes.

5. The passata sauce can now be poured in together with the Italian dried herbs and again mix everything well together, pop on the lid and allow to bubble gently.

6. After 5 minutes, transfer to the simmering oven and allow to cook there for 2 hours.

7. Once the mince is cooked, it is time to assemble the lasagne.

8. Take a large baking dish and put a layer of the Venison mince sauce at the bottom, cover with lasagne sheets and then pour over enough bechamel sauce to cover the sheets well. Take half the cheddar cheese and sprinkle over the top. Repeat the process adding the mince mixture on top, a further layer of pasta, bechamel then top with the remaining cheddar cheese and then the parmesan cheese.

9. Pop in the baking oven for 40 minutes until the top is brown and bubbling. If you think it is browning too fast cover with foil.

10. Serve with garlic bread, salad, red wine and plenty of chatter.

Page 163

Page 167

Page 168

Page 171

Shoulder

Shoulder is a fabulous cut of Venison and should be cooked for many hours at a low temperature so the simmering oven of the Aga works brilliantly for these recipes, as does a slow cooker. I have had great fun playing around with these recipes and I am sure you and your family will love them. Some of the recipes do have a long list of ingredients but the actual cooking part is super simple and of course, always scrumptious.

Venison Sharing Platter with Noodles

Serves 6 people

- 1kg Venison rolled shoulder
- 2 tbsp olive oil
- 1 tbsp butter
- 4 onions, halved in circles
- 1 garlic bulb, each clove peeled but kept whole
- 3 limes
- 500ml boiling water

Dressing

- ¼ tsp cornflour
- 200ml soy sauce
- 1 tsp Lazy Ginger
- 1 tsp Lazy Chilli
- 200g runny honey
- 6 tbsp fish sauce
- 1 tbsp fresh coriander, finely chopped

Salad

- 700g noodles
- 3 tbsp olive oil
- 2 carrots peeled into ribbons
- ½ cucumber peeled into ribbons
- 150g edame beans
- 100g cooked peas
- 1 lime
- Fresh basil, a bunch finely chopped
- Fresh mint, a bunch finely chopped
- Fresh coriander, a bunch finely chopped

Method:

1. Take the Venison shoulder, pop it on a board and smear over the butter and olive oil. Insert the cloves of garlic by piercing holes over the shoulder and inserting the whole cloves. Place the halved onions on the base of a deep roasting tin and put the shoulder on top. Pop in the roasting oven for half an hour, remove and turn the shoulder over then pour over the juice of the 3 limes, the fish sauce and soy sauce. Pour the water into the base of the dish, cover with a tight fitting lid or foil and place in the simmering oven for 3 hours.

2. Remove from the simmering oven and baste the meat – add more water if necessary. Replace in the simmering oven for a further 2 hours or until meat is falling apart.

3. Now make the dressing – put cornflour into a little pan, add in the soy sauce, add the Lazy Ginger and fish sauce and simmer until thick. Add in the tablespoon of finely chopped coriander and the Lazy Chilli then remove from the heat.

4. Cook the noodles per the packet instructions.

5. Mix the salad ingredients together and arrange on a platter. Add the cooked noodles.

6. Pull the meat off the joint using 2 forks and arrange over the noodles.

7. Drizzle over the dressing, squeeze over the lime and add wedges around the edge. Finally scatter over any remaining fresh herbs.

8. Pour the Rosé and enjoy!

Venison Rolled Shoulder with Parsnips and Pepper

For 4 people you will need:

- 1kg Venison rolled shoulder
- 2 tbsp olive oil
- 8 potatoes peeled and chopped into quarters
- 6 parsnips peeled and cut into chunks
- 1 tbsp garlic puree
- Rosemary, a bunch
- 2 tsp paprika
- 2 tsp Bo Tree white Kampot pepper pearls
- 2 tsp Bo Tree Kampot red pepper
- 600ml beef stock

Glaze

- 2 tbsp wholegrain mustard
- 2 tbsp honey

Method:

1. First mix the glaze ingredients together in a bowl and set aside.
2. Pop the quartered potatoes and parsnips into the base of a baking tray, drizzle with oil and salt then place the Venison shoulder on top
3. Mix the garlic puree, paprika and the peppers with the olive oil in a small bowl and cover the shoulder well. Now top with the rosemary.
4. Cover tightly with foil or a lid
5. Pop in the roasting oven for 30 minutes then remove, baste then add the boiling stock to the base of the tray and transfer to the simmering oven for 4 hours keeping the foil or lid on tightly
6. Remove from the oven and pop on the glaze. Replace in the simmering oven for a further hour.
7. When ready to serve, pull the meat apart with 2 forks and enjoy with the scrumptious potato and parsnip mash from the base of the baking tray.

Garlicky Venison Shoulder

Serves 6 people

- 1kg Venison rolled shoulder
- 2 tbsp olive oil
- 1 onion, halved and cut into thin slices
- 1 garlic bulb, peeled
- 3 tsp dried thyme
- 600ml chicken stock

Marinade

- 6 garlic cloves, peeled and crushed
- 3 tbsp olive oil
- 4 tbsp Dijon mustard
- 4 tbsp ground cumin
- 1 tbsp pepper

Garlic Sauce

- 2 tbsp olive oil
- 2 red onions, finely diced
- 4 garlic cloves, peeled and crushed
- 1 red pepper, finely diced
- 3 tbsp fish sauce
- 2 limes, the juice and rind

Method:

1. First, make the garlic sauce by mixing all the ingredients together and set it aside.

2. Now, let's make the marinade by mixing the marinade ingredients together and then rub it all over the Venison shoulder.

3. Take the whole garlic cloves and insert them in cuts all over the shoulder. Marinade for at least 4 hours.

4. When ready to cook, ensure the meat is at room temperature. Heat 3 tablespoons of olive oil in a heavy based pan (with a lid) and brown the Venison shoulder all over. Remove it from the pan and place on a warmed baking tray in the simmering oven.

5. Pour in 2 more tablespoons of olive oil into the pan and scatter in the sliced onions. Add in the hot stock and bring to the boil.

6. Pop the Venison shoulder on top, and sprinkle over the thyme and put on the lid.

7. Ensure it is bubbling then pop it in the simmering oven for 5 hours until the meat is falling apart. You can baste it sporadically and turn it during cooking if you wish.

8. Serve the garlic sauce on the side as a condiment.

Moroccan Venison Rolled Shoulder

This is delicious so don't be put off by the fact you need to marinade it overnight – on the day of cooking, it is so easy and requires minimum action so you can just leave it to cook happily while you enjoy a glass of something scrumptious with your friends!

Serves 6 people

- 1kg Venison rolled shoulder
- 3 tbsp olive oil
- 1 tsp Lazy Chilli
- 4 garlic cloves, peeled and crushed
- 6 garlic cloves, peeled and left whole
- 1 tsp ground cumin
- 2 tbsp light brown sugar
- 3 oranges cut into circles
- 3 shallots, halved in circles
- 10 dried apricots cut into small pieces
- 600ml beef stock

Method:

1. Take the Venison shoulder and use a knife to pierce holes all over and insert the garlic cloves.

2. Place the apricots, ginger, chilli, crushed garlic, cumin and sugar in a bowl then mix well. Rub this mixture all over the venison and leave to marinade overnight.

3. Ensure the Venison is at room temperature before cooking so take it out of the fridge in plenty time.

4. Arrange the onion and orange circles at the bottom of an ovenproof dish (which has a tight- fitting lid) and place the rolled shoulder on top. Drizzle over the olive oil and place in the roasting oven for half an hour.

5. Remove the Venison, baste it well then turn it over, pour the boiling stock into the base of the dish, cover tightly with foil or a lid and place in the simmering oven for 4 hours. You can baste it after 2 hours if you wish. Turn the shoulder over and replace in the simmering oven for a further hour.

6. Serve with cous cous, roasted red onions and sweet potato.

Vibrant Venison Feast

Now, this is a bit of a faff, I won't pretend otherwise, but if you are in the mood for cooking and preparing a real feast for friends then this is definitely worth all the effort. Once it is made, and you have popped it on the serving plates and have all the rice and coleslaw on display, it looks super and your family and friends will adore it.

For 8 people, you will need:

For the Venison:

- 1.4kg Venison rolled shoulder
- 8 tbsp Jerk seasoning
- 4 tsp dried thyme
- 5 spring onions, finely chopped
- 3 tbsp soy sauce
- 6 tbsp runny honey
- 3 limes, juice and zest
- 2 tsp ground ginger
- 600ml boiling water

For the Rice:

- 1 can kidney beans, drained and rinsed
- 1 can sweetcorn
- 1 can full fat coconut milk
- 6 spring onions, finely sliced
- 1 tbsp dried thyme
- 3 garlic cloves, peeled and crushed
- 600g white rice
- 1 tbsp fresh coriander, chopped to garnish

For the coleslaw:

- 1/2 a red cabbage
- 2 red onions finely sliced
- 2 carrots
- 4 tbsp mayonnaise
- 2 limes, juice and rind
- Fresh coriander to garnish

Method:

1. Deal with the Venison first so mix together the Jerk seasoning, thyme, spring onions, soy sauce, honey, lime juice and zest and ginger. Rub this marinade all over the venison, cover with cling film and pop in the fridge for as long as possible, preferably overnight. When you are ready to cook it, ensure you have taken it out of the fridge in plenty time so it is at room temperature.

2. Pop the Venison in a deep oven tray and put in the roasting oven for 30 minutes then remove, turn it over, baste and add the water to the base of the tray. Cover tightly with foil and pop in the simmering oven for 5 hours basting occasionally.

3. Now for the rice so pop the kidney beans, sweetcorn, coconut milk, half the spring onions, thyme, garlic and rice in a large pan on the simmering plate and cover with water. Bring it to a simmer, put on the lid and place in the simmering oven until the rice is cooked.

4. For the coleslaw, pop the cabbage and carrots in a food processor to shred them. Tip them into a bowl and add the onions, lime juice, zest then the mayonnaise. Mix well, garnish with coriander and set aside.

5. Once the Venison is ready, shred the meat using 2 forks.

6. Place the rice on a serving platter, top with the Venison and put the coleslaw around the edges in gentle little heaps.

7. Drizzle over extra lime juice, zest and coriander.

Page 175

Page 176

Page 179

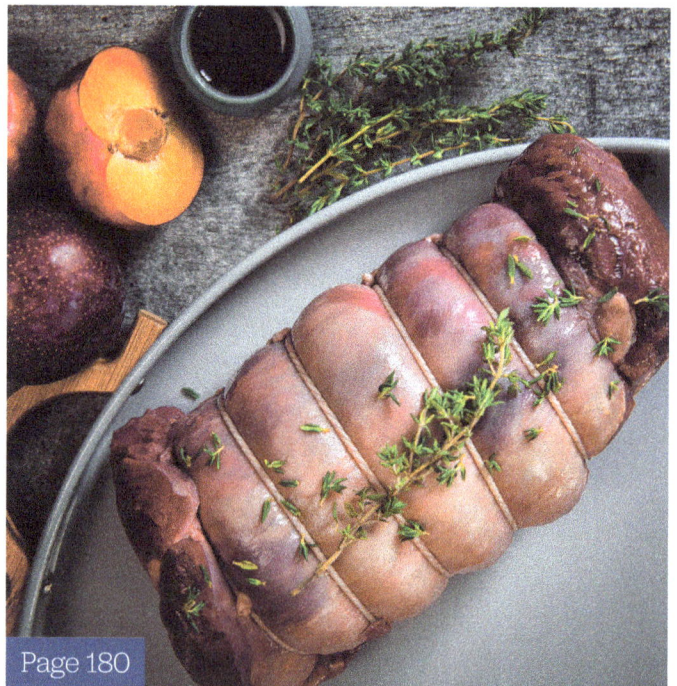
Page 180

Haunch

Haunches are a fabulous way to feed lots of hungry people or as a Sunday treat for the family so the leftovers can be used for a meal the next day which is always a bonus. Although a Venison haunch roast works beautifully with traditional flavours such as juniper berries, it is equally scrumptious with ingredients from Asia and beyond. Don't be scared to experiment.

The timings I have recommended will ensure the Venison is rare so you may need to adjust the cooking times for your family – add on an extra 5 minutes at each stage if you prefer your meat well done.

These recipes use a boneless rolled haunch of Venison but some people do prefer to cook with a haunch which has the bone left in. Please remember that these will cook quicker so deduct 2 or 3 minutes at each stage to ensure your meat remains red and succulent.

Aromatic Roast Haunch of Venison

For 6 people you will need

- 1kg boneless rolled haunch of Venison
- 3 tbsp olive oil
- 1 tsp thyme
- 1 tbsp oregano
- 3 cloves of garlic, peeled and crushed
- $\frac{1}{2}$ tsp ground ginger
- 250ml ginger ale
- 100ml boiling water
- 1 tbsp celery leaves, finely chopped
- 1 tbsp fresh parsley, finely chopped

Aromatic Sauce

- 1 heaped tsp of cornflour
- 200ml cold water
- 1 onion, finely diced
- 3 celery sticks, finely diced
- 3 tsp Thai fish sauce
- 2 tbsp runny honey
- 250ml ginger ale

Method:

1. Mix the crushed garlic, thyme and oregano with 2 tablespoons of olive oil. Rub the mixture over the haunch then sprinkle over the ground ginger. Leave to marinade for as long as possible.

2. Put 200ml of cold water in a mug and add 1 heaped teaspoon of cornflour, mix well until it is cloudy and set it aside.

3. When ready to cook, ensure the meat is at room temperature then take a deep metal roasting tray, pop in 1 tablespoon of olive oil and heat it on the hot plate. Once hot, brown the haunch on both sides – this may take 5 minutes or so on each side.

4. Cover the tray tightly with foil and pop it in the roasting oven for 20 minutes then remove the meat from the oven, peel back the foil and add in the boiling water and 250ml of ginger ale to the base of the tray. Turn the meat over, cover the tray with foil again and move to the baking oven for a further 20 minutes.

5. Remove the meat from the tray and leave to rest on a warm plate.

6. Now, make the sauce. Put the metal tray on the simmering plate, add the cornflour mixture and mix well scraping up all delicious bits from the bottom of the tray. Add in the diced onion, celery, another 250ml of ginger ale, the fish sauce, runny honey and mix well. Allow to bubble gently for 10 minutes.

7. Slice the meat, place on a platter and cover with the sauce and sprinkle over the celery leaves and fresh parsley. Serve with lots of creamy mashed potato.

Roast Haunch of Venison with Garlic

For true domestic god or goddess status, do add carrots and parsnips and extra onions to the base of the roasting tin so that the veg and meat all cooks together – the juice from the venison will really enhance all the flavours.

For 6 people you will need:

- 1kg boneless rolled haunch of Venison
- 2 tbsp olive oil
- 2 sprigs fresh rosemary
- 4 onions, cut in half
- 500ml beef stock
- 10 garlic cloves
- Freshly milled pepper

Method:

1. Take your Venison haunch and rub 2 tablespoons of olive oil all over it.
2. Using a sharp knife, pierce the haunch 10 times and insert a clove of garlic into each little hole.
3. Sprinkle over the freshly milled pepper liberally.
4. Get a roasting dish with a tight-fitting lid (like Le Cresuet) and place the halved onions at the bottom and pop the roast haunch on top.
5. Put the fresh rosemary on top.
6. Place the Venison in the roasting oven for 20 mins and allow it to brown.
7. Now add the hot stock to the pan, pop on a tight-fitting lid and transfer to the baking oven for 20 minutes, basting half way through.
8. Remove from the heat and rest the haunch on a board before carving.
9. Serve with dauphinoise potatoes and lots of roasted vegetables.

Venison Haunch with Port

This is a wonderful Sunday roast recipe to be enjoyed with horseraddish, extra roasted vegetables and of course friends and family.

For 8 people you will need

- 1.5kg boneless rolled haunch of Venison
- 3 tbsp olive oil
- 1 tbsp butter
- 600g of beetroot cut into chunks
- 4 sprigs of thyme
- 10 juniper berries, crushed in a pestle and mortar
- 5 red onions, halved and cut into chunks
- 300ml port
- 1 tbsp freshly chopped parsley

For the gravy

- 2 tsp dried thyme
- 4 juniper berries, crushed in a pestle and mortar
- 4 garlic cloves, peeled and crushed
- 4 tbsp redcurrant jelly (if you were cooking this after Christmas and had Cranberry Sauce left over then do use that)
- 600ml beef stock
- 1 tsp freshly chopped parsley

Method:

1. Put the beetroot wedges and red onions in a deep metal roasting tin with half the thyme and drizzle with 1 tablespoon of olive oil then mix well. Cover with foil and roast for 20 minutes in the hot roasting oven then pop the vegetables into a warmed bowl and place this in the simmering oven.

2. Rub the crushed juniper berries all over the Venison haunch. Now, put the roasting tin on the heat and add in 2 tablespoons of olive oil. Add the Venison haunch and brown the meat on both sides.

3. Add back the beetroot and red onions to the roasting dish and ensure the meat is on top of the veg. Pop the butter on top of the haunch and scatter over the remaining thyme.

4. Now, pour the port into base of the tin and cover tightly with foil.

5. Pop in the roasting oven for 20 minutes, remove then baste the meat, re-cover and pop into baking oven for a further 20 minutes.

6. Remove the Venison from the heat and let it rest on a board. Remove the vegetables and keep them warm in the simmering oven in a bowl.

7. Put the metal roasting tin on the hot plate and add the gravy ingredients, mix well and allow it to simmer gently.

8. Slice the Venison and serve with the vegetables on a large platter. Pour the gravy over the top. Scatter over the fresh parsley and enjoy with potato wedges, friends and red wine.

Thyme Venison with Plum Gravy

We love this recipe as it is a really easy Sunday lunch and we always have lots of plum compote in the freezer so adding this to the gravy gives it extra texture and depth of flavour. We also like to add the onions (which the venison has roasted on) to the gravy having cut them into chunks.

For 6 people you will need:

- 1kg boneless rolled haunch of Venison
- 3 tbsp olive oil
- 1 bulb of garlic, peeled
- 1 large bunch of fresh thyme
- 2 onions cut in half to make thick circles
- 3 tbsp Worcestershire sauce
- 100ml hot water

For the gravy

- 1 glass of red wine (as a bottle is open you may as well have a glass as you cook)
- 1 tbsp beef gravy granules
- 600ml beef stock
- 2 tbsp of plum jam or compote

Method:

1. Place the onion circles at the bottom of a large roasting pan, sprinkle with olive oil and pop the haunch on top.

2. Season the meat then insert peeled garlic cloves all over the meat using a sharp knife to make little holes.

3. Take the thyme and add in small sprigs to the little garlic holes. Have a glass of red wine - just to try it.

4. Sprinkle the haunch with the Worcestershire sauce.

5. Pop the Venison into the roasting oven for 20 minutes until brown then remove and baste. Add 100ml of hot water to the base, cover tightly with a lid or foil and place in the baking oven for 20 minutes.

6. Remove the Venison from the oven, pop the meat onto a dish and place in the plate warming oven of the Aga.

7. Pop the roasting tin on the hot plate, add the wine and bring to the boil scraping all the bits from the bottom to add delicious flavour to the gravy.

8. Once it has reduced by half, add in the gravy granules, mix well and move to the simmering plate. Now add in the stock a little at a time whisking well and watch it thicken. Add in the plum jam or compote until it is glossy. I would now add in the cut up roasted onions from the bottom of the roasting dish too. Yum.

9. Slice the Venison and serve with delicious roasties, green beans and lashings of red wine which you have already opened for the gravy – it would be rude not to.

Page 185

Page 186

Page 190

Page 193

Venison Fillet

Undoubtedly fillet is the best cut of Venison and does not require much cooking at all. Sometimes referred to as backstrap or loin, it is incredibly versatile and can be used with any of the sauces in this book. It cooks beautifully on the BBQ and of course, as it cooks so quickly and easily, do remember our Golden Rule of less is more. Always undercook the Venison and leave it to rest on a board. Keep your stop watch handy as I find this the best way to ensure a perfect fillet each and every time.

Filet Mignon is the gorgeous little fillet which lies in behind the larger fillet. It is succulent and delicious but quite small so feeds 2 to 3 people.

The general rule is to allow 125g of fillet per person but as always, this will depend on who you are feeding!

Simple Venison Fillet

Venison fillet is such a treat and although easy to cook, it always looks very impressive. We enjoy it rare so do remember that when considering your timings.

For 4 people you will need:

- 500g of Venison fillet
- 2 tbsp olive oil
- 1 tbsp Bo Tree Kampot black pepper
- 1 tbspBo Tree Kampot red pepper

Method:

1. Drizzle the olive oil onto a large plate or board then scatter the pepper over it and mix it all together.

2. Roll the fillet in the pepper mixture to ensure it is evenly coated and leave to marinade for as long as possible.

3. Before cooking, ensure the fillet is at room temperature.

4. Heat a heavy based pan until smoking and cook the meat on both side for 4 minutes.

5. Leave to rest for 8 minutes or so before slicing.

We enjoy this with salad in the Summer or dauphinoise potatoes and roasted vegetables in the Winter.

Creamy Venison Fillet

Here is a scrumptious fillet recipe with a sauce everyone will adore to get you started but really, once you are cooking fillets confidently, you can serve them with anything you fancy, from a simple garlic mayonnaise to a more complex sauce with richer flavours.

For 4 people you will need:

- 500g of Venison fillet
- 2 tbsp olive oil
- 2 shallots, finely diced
- 1 red onion, halved and finely sliced
- 300ml double cream
- 2 tbsp of French grainy mustard
- Handful of chopped fresh parsley

Method:

1. Put 1 tablespoon of olive oil in a frying pan on the hot plate and add the shallots and onions. Move the pan to the simmering plate, and allow them to soften slowly stirring gently. Transfer them to a bowl and place in the simmering oven.

2. Move the pan back to the hot plate, add the other tablespoon of olive oil to the empty frying pan and when it is hot add the fillet, sealing it on each side for 4 minutes then remove it from the pan and place it on a board to rest.

3. Add the grainy mustard to the frying pan, stirring in all the delicious bits from the bottom of the pan. When warm, add in the cream and stir well ensuring it heats up gently. Add the onions to the pan and mix well.

4. Cut the fillet into slices, arrange on the plate then top with the warm creamy mustard sauce, scatter the fresh parsley over it and serve immediately with a scrumptious glass of red, friends and chatter.

Venison Fillet with Berries

This Summer recipe uses berries which can be from the garden or the fridge. It looks pretty impressive so is a perfect dinner party dish and can be cooked last minute with a glass in hand as you chat to friends or even better, it could be a romantic meal for 2. I use honeyberry jam here which is absolutely scrumptious but you could use any jam you prefer.

For 4 people you will need:

- 500g Venison fillet
- 2 tbsp olive oil
- 1 tbsp balsamic vinegar
- 150ml beef stock
- 2 tbsp honeyberry jam
- 2 garlic cloves, peeled and crushed
- 100g of raspberries, blueberries, honeyberries or blackberries

Method:

1. Place the fillet on a board and cover in the balsamic vinegar. Leave it for an hour or so and ensure the Venison is at room temperature before cooking.

2. Heat the olive oil in a frying pan on the hot plate and when hot, pan fry the venison for 4 minutes on each side then remove then place on a board and leave to rest.

3. Take the empty pan and add in the stock, honeyberry jam, crushed garlic and heat quickly on the hot plate stirring constantly.

4. Once it has thickened, move to the simmering plate, add the fresh berries and stir until they are soft.

5. Slice the Venison fillet, arrange on the plates and top with the sauce.

6. For full indulgence serve with dauphinoise potatoes or little new potato roasties.

Venison Fillet with Plum Sauce

I like this recipe as I use plums from the garden that look slightly past their best - they are at their sweetest and cook quicker.

For 4 people you will need:

- 500g Venison fillet
- 1 tbsp olive oil
- 1 tsp butter
- 2 garlic cloves, peeled and crushed
- 2 tsp juniper berries, crushed in a pestle and mortar
- 6 plums, stoned - 3 finely chopped with skin removed and 3 cut into quarters
- 4 tbsp whiskey
- 150ml beef stock

Method:

1. Marinade the Venison covered with the crushed juniper berries for at least 3 hours before cooking.

2. Heat the butter and olive oil in a non stick frying pan on the hot plate until it is really hot.

3. Add the quartered plums and the Venison to the pan and sear the Venison on the hot plate for 4 minutes either side then remove the fillet and plums from the heat and leave to rest on a board.

4. Now move the pan to the simmering plate, add the other plums and crushed garlic into the empty Venison pan and cook gently until really soft. Pour in the whiskey and hot stock. Allow it to bubble happily for 10 minutes so the sauce thickens.

5. Once the plums are super soft, remove the mixture from the heat.

6. Slice the Venison and arrange it on the plates, top with the plum quarters and the sauce. Yum!

Venison Carpaccio

This is a very special recipe which appears a bit of a faff, and yes there are various stages to it, but I promise it is worth it! You do not need much Venison per person as this is really a starter or a nibble so it does make an expensive cut of meat go further.

For 6 - 8 people you will need:

- 350g Venison filet mignon
- 2 tsp juniper berries, crushed in a pestle and mortar
- 2 tbsp dried thyme
- 3 tsp freshly ground black pepper
- 6 tbsp gin
- 3 tbsp caster sugar
- 4 tbsp pink salt

Method:

1. Crush the juniper berries and mix with the freshly ground pepper and dried thyme.

2. Rub this mixture all over the filet mignon ensuring it is well coated and pop it in a large zip lock bag.

3. Now, mix the gin, sugar and salt together in a jug and pour this mixture into the bag making sure the Venison is well covered with the gin mixture.

4. Seal the bag tightly, removing as much air as possible and pop the bag into a dish and place it the fridge for 2 days. Turn the meat 3 times a day to ensure the Venison is in the gin mixture and well covered on all sides.

5. Remove the Venison from the fridge, take it out the bag and drain off the gin. Bring the meat to room temperature.

6. Take a griddle pan and pop it on the hot plate. When it is really hot, sear the fillet in the pan for a minute only on each side.

7. Remove the meat from the pan and place it on a board. Once it has cooled, wrap it tightly in cling film, freeze for 2 hours then remove and slice the meat as thinly as you can.

8. Serve immediately.

Sauces

Venison steaks, minute steaks and fillets are all so easy to cook in griddle pans and on the BBQ so once you have mastered the art of cooking these and have built your confidence, these sauces are perfect to serve with them to vary the dish according to the occasion.

They are all super easy to make and of course utterly scrumptious – so here are a collection my family's favourites for you to enjoy which cover all seasons and use readily available ingredients.

Cherry Sauce

Ingredients

- 12 cherries – stones out
- 50g caster sugar
- 3 tbsp red wine vinegar
- 400ml chicken stock
- 175ml red wine
- 1 tsp redcurrant jam

Method

1. Take a non-stick saucepan and add the sugar and red wine vinegar in pan on the hot plate and reduce by boiling it rapidly.
2. Add the wine and stock then reduce by 2/3rds.
3. Move the pan to the simmering plate, add the stoned cherries and jam and allow it to simmer gently for 3 minutes.
4. Taste the sauce and if it needs more sweetness then add another teaspoon of jam, mixing it well into the sauce.

Port Sauce

Ingredients

- 2 onions, finely diced
- 300ml port
- 1 tbsp grainy French mustard
- 300ml double cream
- Seasoning

Method

1. Heat a non-stick saucepan on the simmering plate, and add the diced onions and port and simmer until reduced by half.
2. Stir in the mustard and double cream, gently warm then season and serve.

Chimichurri Sauce

Ingredients

- 1 tbsp olive oil
- 2 crushed garlic cloves
- 1 tbsp fresh parsley, chopped
- 1 tbsp fresh mint, chopped
- 1 tsp Lazy Chilli
- 3 tbsp lime juice

Method

Simply mix the ingredients together in a bowl, season to taste and serve as a condiment.

Tarragon Sauce

Ingredients

- 1 tsp butter
- 1 packet of fresh tarragon, finely chopped
- 2 shallots, finely diced
- $\frac{1}{2}$ tsp red pepper
- 1 glass Rosé wine
- 4 tablespoons double cream

Method

1. Put the butter in a non-stick saucepan on the simmering plate and when it has melted, add the shallots and gently soften.
2. Add in the red pepper and mix well.
3. Stir in the glass of wine, bubble and reduce by half.
4. Add in the finely chopped tarragon and stir well.
5. Slowly pour in the double cream, stirring gently.
6. Season and serve warm as a condiment.

Greek Sauce

Ingredients

- 1 tbsp olive oil
- 2 tbsp lemon juice
- 1 tbsp oregano
- 1 lemon - zest

Method

1. Mix all the ingredients together and season to taste.
2. Drizzle over the cooked Venison steaks or fillet for a lovely summery zing.

Bacon & Onion Sauce

Ingredients

- 1 tsp olive oil
- 1 onion, finely diced
- 100g streaky dry cured bacon cubed
- 2 shallots finely chopped
- 150ml red wine
- 150ml beef stock

Method

1. In a wide based pan, pour in the olive oil and fry the onions and bacon on the hot plate until brown.
2. Add the shallots, wine and stock, mixing well.
3. Allow it to bubble and reduce until the sauce is glossy and thick and then season to taste.

Coriander Sauce

Ingredients

- 1 bunch of fresh coriander, finely chopped
- 3 shallots, finely diced
- 1 tsp Dijon mustard
- 2 tbsp full fat mayonnaise
- 1 tbsp Greek yoghurt
- 2 tbsp double cream
- Pinch of cayenne pepper

Method

1. Mix the coriander, shallots and Dijon mustard together in a bowl.
2. In a separate bowl, mix the mayonnaise, yoghurt, cream and cayenne pepper together.
3. Mix both bowls together gently and serve.

Dill Sauce

Ingredients

- 1 pot of full fat crème fraiche
- 1 shallot, finely diced
- 2 tbsp dill, finely chopped
- 2 lemons, just the juice
- ½ tsp ground coriander

Method

1. Put the shallots and lemon juice in a bowl and mix well ensuring all the shallots are covered in the juice.
2. Add in the dill and coriander then mix well.
3. Leave for 30 minutes so the lemon juice can soften the shallots then add in the crème fraiche and mix together. Season to taste and serve.

Thank You

Writing this book has been such an exciting, creative process and I have loved every minute of it. I am so grateful to my family for trying endless concoctions of flavours, eating multiple versions of the same recipe so I could get it just right, and for always giving honest feedback (even if I didn't want to hear it!).

My husband Jeremy is a constant support and I love him dearly – thank you for helping me make my dreams come true and for being my partner in fun and laughter. My gorgeous daughters Kinvara and Jemima have been superb sous chefs behind the scenes, so helpful on photo shoot days and always so kind to me, I love you both so much, thank you for being you.

My mother Margaret and dear friend Emily Saunders have been so kind reading endless pages of recipe ingredients and methodology descriptions so I could get everything as perfect as possible – thank you both so much, I am eternally grateful for your help, support and words of encouragement.

Mark at oomph! Design has been wonderful – a huge thank you for bringing the book to life and for your endless patience with my edits, you are a star.

To the fabulous Louise and Kyle at Hamilton Kerr Photography, a huge thank you for your creativity with the photographs and for interpreting what I was aiming to achieve so brilliantly. Despite all the hard work in preparation of each photo shoot day, I absolutely loved them and miss that creative process with you already.

Finally, to all of you, my lovely readers who have bought this book – "thank you" for deciding to give Venison a try. I hope you all enjoy making these simple, scrumptious recipes and I know your family and friends will love you for feeding them so well!

Anona x

www.ingramcontent.com/pod-product-compliance
Lightning Source LLC
Chambersburg PA
CBHW061227150426

42812CB00054BA/2535